Super
Science
Concoctions

ISBN-13: 978-0-8249-6803-8 (softcover)
ISBN-13: 978-0-8249-6802-1 (hardcover)

Published by Williamson Books
An imprint of Ideals Publications
A Guideposts Company
535 Metroplex Drive, Suite 250
Nashville, Tennessee 37211
www.idealsbooks.com

Printed and bound in China

Library of Congress Cataloging-in-Publication Data
Hauser, Jill Frankel, 1950–
       Super science concoctions: 50 mysterious mixtures for fabulous fun/Jill Frankel Hauser.
       p. cm. — "A Williamson kids can! book."
       Includes index.
       Summary: Over 75 safe, inexpensive science experiments with mixtures that illustrate changes in form and
       chemical composition.

       1. Science—Experiments—Juvenile literature.
       2. Mixtures—Experiments—Juvenile literature.
       3. Phase rule and equilibrium—Experiments—Juvenile literature. 4. Scientific recreations—Juvenile literature.
       [1. Science—Experiments. 2. Mixtures—Experiments. 3. Experiments.] I. Title.
Q164.H38 1997
500.2'078—dc20
                                                95-47894
                                                  CIP
                                                  AC

10 9 8 7 6 5 4 3 2 1

Kids Can!® Series Editor: Susan Williamson
Design: Georgina Chidlow-Rucker
Kids Can!® is a registered trademark of Ideals Publications.

To my father, Melvin Frankel, my first mentor, through whom science gave birth to perpetual
wonder and the reality of this book became possible.

Thank you "Sir" Danny Abbott, Shasta High's famous (infamous?) whiz-bang chemistry instructor of
27 years. Put me in line with that procession of students who gave you handshakes, hugs, and
accolades on the last day of school for making a difficult subject crystal clear.

Super Science Concoctions

50 Mysterious Mixtures for Fabulous Fun

By Jill Frankel Hauser

Illustrations by Michael Kline

williamsonbooks™

Nashville, Tennessee

Contents

Welcome To Your Kitchen Laboratory!

There are fantastic things just waiting to happen—using the chemicals found right in your kitchen cabinet. That's right! No need to buy a chemistry set! The concoctions you create will help you unlock the most amazing secrets of science.

Are you curious to learn why gelatin jiggles? Would you like to bounce a plastic blob? How about floating one strange liquid on top of another? Or perhaps you'd like to cook up some sweet, solid foam. If so, then start concocting! Explore the wondrous world of science with mysterious mixtures that creep, bubble, and stretch your knowledge and thinking powers. Each concoction is really a scientific experiment. So, before you begin, learn to think like a scientist.

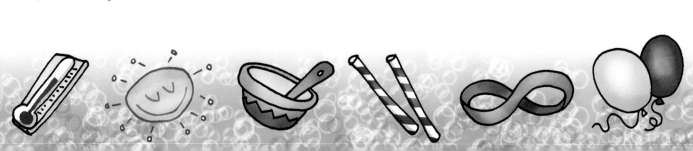

Think Science

Scientists and kids have something important in common: they both wonder why. And they both try to figure things out. Asking questions and finding answers is so important to scientists that they've developed an organized way to do this. It's called the scientific method. Next time you wonder why, try following these easy, yet powerful steps for discovering the answer.

Wonder Why

What do you want to learn about the world? Be curious and think of questions you want to discover the answers to.

Test Your Guess

Think up an experiment that will tell you if your hypothesis is right. Try the experiment.

Take a Guess

What do you think the answer might be? Put your guess into a statement that can be tested. This is called the hypothesis.

Observe and Record

Carefully observe everything that happens during and after your experiment. Make notes about what you observe.

Get Organized

The more organized your data, the more useful it is. You might want to record your observations in the form of a graph, chart, table, or diagram.

What can You Say?

Does the data you collected support your hypothesis? Or does it make you think you should start over? If so, you'll need to think of another possibility and design a new experiment.

If your hypothesis holds up to experimentation, you may be able to come up with a *theory*. A theory is the best possible explanation for the data you collected.

Share The Results

Scientists learn from each other's work. Even though your theory seems true, it may not be. Often new facts are discovered, even many years later, and theories change.

Figuring out answers is a fascinating search that never ends. There's always more to discover.

Science Steps

Ready, Set . . . Wait

Read all instructions first. Make sure you understand what you're about to do. Assemble all ingredients and equipment before starting.

Don't Blink

Watch carefully. One of the most important things scientists do is to observe. Exactly what happens when you combine two chemicals? What do you notice about the way those liquids move? Just how does the new substance you create behave? What colors do you see? How does that blob really feel? Is the odor stronger after one day or one week? The more carefully you observe, the more you learn and the closer you get to discovering answers to your questions.

Stand By

Stay with your experiment from beginning to end, or for longer term experiments, set up an observation schedule. You never know exactly when a change will occur. Sometimes changes happen quickly. Sometimes there are changes, almost too small to notice, happening over many days.

No Such Thing as Failure

If your experiment does not turn out exactly as planned, you can always try it again. Mistakes are usually very valuable learning experiences. Remember, great scientists often fail many times before making important discoveries.

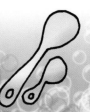

SAFE SCIENCE

- Get permission from a grownup before concocting.

- Have a grownup be your laboratory assistant—especially if the experiment calls for using anything hot or sharp. In this book, look for the hot warning symbol.

- Collect a set of equipment used only for experimenting. Use only plastic containers.

- Make sure all equipment is clean and dry. Wash after use.

- Keep your hands away from mouth and eyes while experimenting. Wash your hands after each experiment.

- Keep younger kids and pets away while experimenting.

- Never taste any concoction or the ingredients used unless it is specifically stated that you are making something to eat. In this book, look for the "O.K. to Eat!" symbol. Otherwise, do not taste!

- Use safety goggles when working with substances that might shatter or splatter. Wear an apron to protect clothes.

- Label all ingredients you use and concoctions you create.

- Dispose of experiments properly as described in the instructions.

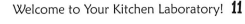

Science Supplies

All the concoctions in this book are made from safe, inexpensive, easy-to-find household ingredients. Here are some of the items you'll need and where to find them:

GROCERY STORE

- Salt
- Sugar
- Cornstarch
- Flour
- Baking soda
- Vinegar
- Gelatin
- Food coloring
- Eggs
- Liquid dishwashing soap
- Cooking oil
- Chocolate chips
- Red cabbage
- Borax
- Paraffin

DRUG STORE

- Rubbing alcohol
- Epsom salts
- Medicine dropper (to make your own, see page 13)

HARDWARE STORE

- White glue
- Hot glue
- Corks
- Plaster of Paris

CRAFT STORE

- Art paper
- Powdered tempera paint
- Felt-tip pens
- Pipe cleaners

AROUND THE HOUSE

- Measuring spoons and cups
- Mixing container and spoon
- Drinking straws
- Water
- Ice cubes
- Stove
- Plastic storage containers with lids
- Coffee filters
- Waxed paper
- String
- Clear film canisters

Making a Science Lab

Basic laboratory equipment can either be found around the house or made.

Test Tubes

You only need to combine small amounts of chemicals to observe the results. That's why scientists use test tubes. You can use:

- Clear film canisters. The clear ones are hard to come by. Ask for them at photo shops and be persistent.
- Clear floral vials often used for roses.
- Test tubes purchased from science or hobby shops. Be careful as these break easily.

Test Tube Rack

Set a small, empty cracker box on its side. Trace around the top of your test tube to make holes the right size to hold the tubes. Cut out the holes. Cut a window into side of box.

Dropper

Dip a drinking straw in a glass of water. Press your finger down over the top while lifting the straw from the glass. Water remains trapped inside. Lift, then quickly replace your finger to let one drop fall. Practice until you can let one drop fall at a time.

Science Log

Spiral notebook with blank lined or unlined pages.

Beakers and Vials

Collect clear plastic food containers of all sizes and measuring spoons and cups.

Labels

Use self-adhesive labels to identify all chemicals (ingredients) and experiments.

Strange-but-True Brews

Moving molecules, mixed-up molecules, and molecules just joining together are the basis for concocting these amazing brews.

So what's a molecule, you ask? Just think of a drop of water. If you were to divide that drop into the tiniest droplet possible and still have actual water, that particle would be called a molecule—in this case, a water molecule.

The *chemical formula* for water—H_2O—tells you something about its make-up. If you could further divide that water molecule, you would discover the even tinier particles from which it is made, but you wouldn't have water anymore. Instead, you'd have two atoms of hydrogen (2H) and one atom of oxygen (O). Each of these atoms can exist by itself as something quite different from the molecule of water formed when they combine. In fact, hydrogen is an explosive gas and oxygen is the gas we breathe to survive!

The concoctions in this section explore miraculous molecules. Watch them move, mix, and un-mix right before your eyes!

SCIENCE SPEAK

MOLECULE OR ATOM?

A *molecule* is the smallest particle of a substance that is still that same kind of substance. It's made of atoms—atoms that by themselves may not be at all like a molecule of the substance they combine to create.

An *atom*, on the other hand, is the smallest particle of a substance that can exist by itself. In fact, the word atom in Greek means "uncuttable." Now you know why.

MoLecuLe

water

AToms

Scientific Salad Dressings

If you soak garlic in olive oil, or herbs in vinegar, you'll discover how flavorful molecules can transform ordinary liquids into great gourmet dressings! Enjoy scientific dressings on your favorite salad.

What You Need
- **Olive oil**
- **Whole garlic cloves**
- **Clean bottles with tight-fitting lids**
- **Vinegar**
- **Fresh herb sprigs such as rosemary, thyme, sage, tarragon, dill, or dried herbs**

What You Do

To make garlic oil:

1 Smell the oil; then smell the garlic. Place about six garlic cloves in a bottle and fill with olive oil.

2 Insert a cork or screw on the top tightly.

3 Let the flavor develop for about two days in a cool, dark place. How do you think the oil will smell now? Store oil in the refrigerator.

To make herb vinegar:

1 Smell the vinegar. Smell the herb of your choice. Then put about three fresh herb sprigs in a bottle. Fill the bottle with vinegar.

2 Insert a cork or screw on the top tightly.

3 Let the flavor develop for about ten days in a cool, dark place. How do you think the vinegar will smell now?

SOLVENT OR SOLUTE?

A *solution* is a special kind of liquid mixture. When you stir sugar into water, you make a solution. When you stir sand into water, you won't make a solution. That's because the sugar *dissolves* and spreads evenly throughout the water, but the sand settles at the bottom, never dissolving in the water.

Here's how it works: The tiny molecules of the water force their way between the larger molecules of the sugar. This separates the sugar molecules and causes them to float evenly among the water molecules. Voila . . . a solution! The stuff that dissolves is called the *solute*. The liquid it dissolves into is called a *solvent*.

SolVent (water) + SoLuTe (sugar) = Solution (sugar water)

In your flavored oils, the olive oil (solvent) dissolves the flavor molecules from the garlic (solute). The new product, garlic oil, is similar to the parts from which it's made. It's still an oil, but now it tastes and smells like garlic! The same thing happens to the vinegar and herb mixture. The new solution is wonderfully like both the solvent and the solute.

Oil (Solvent) + Garlic (Solute) = Garlic Oil (Solution)

SUPER FUN! Use your imagination to come up with other delicious flavors. Start with quality vinegars, oils, and fresh herbs. Try the following flavors separately or in combination with another:

- Green onions
- Peppercorns
- Dried chilies
- Bay leaves
- Basil
- Oregano
- Lemon or orange peel (cut in a continuous spiral from clean fruit)
- Mint
- Dill

Flavored oils and vinegars make lovely gifts. Tie a ribbon or twine around the neck of the bottle and label with the flavor and bottling date. Store flavored oils in the refrigerator. (When "bottling" flavored vinegar, first strain the herbs, reserving vinegar; then rinse the bottle. Refill the bottle with the strained vinegar and a fresh sprig of the herb used.)

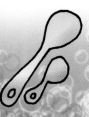

Perfume Chemistry

Alcohol is a good solvent for dissolving the fragrant oil solutes from herbs and flowers. Place one of the following ingredients in a clear film canister: cloves, vanilla bean, cinnamon bark, orange or lemon peel bits, or lavender or rose petals. Cover with 2 tablespoons (30 ml) of rubbing alcohol and secure the lid. Shake once a day for a week. When the solution smells more like the fragrance than the rubbing alcohol, it's ready. Dab the scented rubbing alcohol on your wrist, and smell the fragrance. You've concocted perfume! For stronger scents, replace the solute with a fresh one after a week. Experiment with other solutes to find your favorite scent!

LET'S GET PRACTICAL

IT Makes Scents

It takes 8,000 crushed roses to make just one gram (barely a dab) of rose oil for perfume. But thanks to clever chemists, there's a simpler way to capture a flower's precious fragrance. Scientists are able to analyze the molecules that make up a flower's scent and then artificially reproduce the natural fragrant oils with chemicals in the laboratory. The newly scented solute is dissolved in an unscented solvent. The result is a flower-friendly solution—perfume!

Molecules in Motion

There's no need to stir this solution—the solute dissolves without any help!

What You Need

- **Jar**
- **Water**
- **Food coloring**

What You Do

1 Fill the jar with water.

2 Add a few drops of food coloring. Watch how the drops sink to the bottom, leaving a colored trail.

3 Leave the jar undisturbed. How do you think it will look later in the day? Check back and see if you are right.

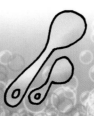

MORE TO EXPLORE

How quickly does the food coloring spread throughout these liquids? Try them and see!

- Ice water
- Hot water
- Brine (see page 75)

Observe what happens in these tasty solutions:

- Add instant drink powder to a glass of cold water.
- Add instant soup powder to a cup of hot water.

The Principle of the Thing

Although you can't see them, water molecules are always on the move. The food coloring particles are bombarded by these watery movers and shakers. Eventually the jar of water is evenly colored without anyone ever stirring the mixture!

In hot water, molecules move even faster. So the coloring spreads more quickly in hot water than in cold. What happens in brine? The spaces between the water molecules are already filled with salt, so the coloring can't spread as quickly.

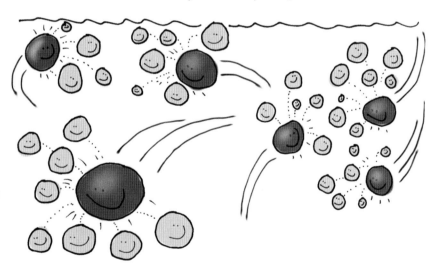

Concoct a Set of Watercolors

Fill film canisters with a little water. Add a few drops of food coloring to each. How quickly does the water become colored? Test the brilliancy of your colorful solutions by painting with them on paper.

On The Move

Molecules are always moving. And thanks to their *molecular motion*, you don't need to bother with a spoon to stir your mixture. Just sit back and let the food coloring *diffuse*, or mix, throughout the water.

LET'S GET PRACTICAL

Movin' and Diffusin'

Can you smell what's cooking for dinner from your bedroom? Those amazing aromas are actually tiny gas molecules on the move! Like liquid molecules, gas molecules are also in motion. In fact, they move even more quickly and further apart from each other.

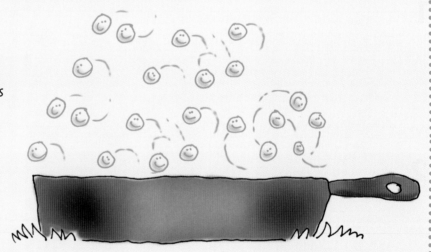

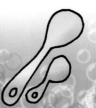

1 + 1 ≠ 2 Brew

When does one plus one not equal two? You'll find the answer as you discover the spaces that lurk between water molecules. Amaze your friends by mixing up this magic trick.

What You Need

- **Clear film canister**
- **Water**
- **Tablespoon**
- **Waterproof marker**
- **Small bowls or cups**
- **Rubbing alcohol**
- **Food coloring**

What You Do

1 Prepare a 2-tablespoon (30 ml) measuring vial by pouring exactly 1 tablespoon (15 ml) of water into a film canister. Mark the level "1." Add a second tablespoon (15 ml) of water and mark the level "2." Dump out the water.

2 Prepare colored water and colored rubbing alcohol by adding a drop or two of different colored food coloring to each liquid.

3 Explain to your audience that you will add 1 tablespoon (15 ml) of each of two mystery liquids to the vial. Ask them to predict the level of the new mixture.

4 Measure 1 tablespoon (15 ml) of colored water and pour it into the vial.

5 Add 1 tablespoon (15 ml) of colored rubbing alcohol. Wave your hands and say, "Abraca-science!" Was their prediction correct? Incredible! The new mixture does not reach the 2-tablespoon (30 ml) level of the vial.

MORE TO EXPLORE

- Fill a 2-cup (500 ml) measuring cup to the 1-cup (250 ml) level with water. Carefully add a spoonful of sugar. Does the water level change? How many spoonfuls can you add before the water level changes? How much salt can you add to 1 cup (250 ml) of water?

- Try this again using hot water. Can you add more or less sugar to hot water without spilling?

Bean Bottles

Make a colorful layered bean jar. Think about the colors and textures you are using. Take a 1-quart or 1-pint glass jar and alternate layers of colorful beans with a layer of salt, cornmeal, or other finely ground dry food. Notice that the salt fills in between the larger beans before it starts to build up a layer. What does this kitchen art remind you of?

Right On, Democritus!

Democritus, a Greek thinker who lived more than 2,000 years ago, believed that all substances were made up of tiny particles with empty spaces in between. That's just what you discovered and what scientists believe today.

The Principle of the Thing

Fill a cup to the brim with pebbles. Can you still add sand without overflowing the cup? Sure. You can easily see how the sand fills the spaces between the pebbles. Something similar happens when you mix water and rubbing alcohol. Because water molecules are loosely packed, the spaces between them make perfect places for rubbing alcohol (or salt or sugar) molecules to fit!

Hot water molecules are even farther apart, so even more sugar molecules can fit into those larger spaces.

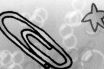

Un-Mixed Mix-Up

Mixing up a solution is easy, but have you ever thought of taking one apart?
Try it with this colorful concoction.

What You Need

- **Jar with lid**
- **Food coloring (red, yellow, blue)**
- **Coffee filter**
- **Scissors**
- **Pencil and paper clips**
- **Water**

What You Do

1 Place a drop of each color of food coloring in the lid. Mix together. What color did you create?

2 Cut a strip from the coffee filter, 1 inch (2.5 cm) wide and a little longer than the height of the jar.

3 Place a dot of the mixed colors about 1 inch (2.5 cm) up from the bottom of the strip.

4 Use the paper clip to secure the other end of the strip to the pencil, as shown.

5 Fill the jar with about ½ inch (1 cm) of water.

6 Dangle the strip in the jar so that just the bottom edge touches the water. Now watch the action.

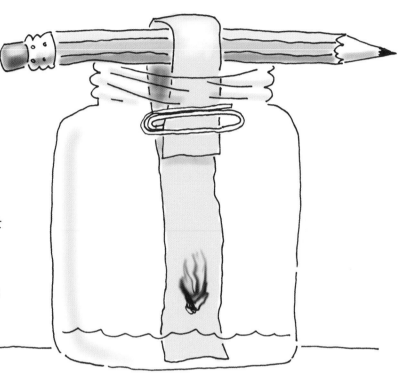

Science Clues

How does the water creep up the filter? For a clue, see Creepy Water Ghosts, page 96.

Un-Mix Felt-Tip Marker Colors

Instead of food coloring, use dots of dark felt-tip marker ink in step 3 on previous page. Use a separate strip for each color. Which colors do you think you'll see travel up the paper? Label each one with the name of the original color used.

Un-Mix Candy Colors

Place several candy-coated chocolates or jelly beans of the same color in a jar. Add a little warm water and swish. Hang coffee filter strips as shown. Do any candy coatings contain more than one color?

Pigment Power

People have used plants to color cloth for thousands of years. You can make these natural dyes too! Tear up bits of the suggested plants in a large pot. Cover with water. Ask a grownup to simmer the concoction for about 15 minutes. When cool, strain the dye from the plant. (Be careful—it will stain your clothing!) Use the dye to color cotton cloth.

Plants to try:

Red: berries, beets

Purple: grape juice concentrate

Brown: onion skins

Green: parsley, spinach

The Principle of the Thing

As the water travels through the paper fibers, it carries the dye along with it. The color in dye comes from pigments. Some dyes contain one pigment; others contain several. Different pigment molecules travel at different speeds so that's why you see separate paths of color.

      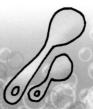 

Dragon Bookmarks

Use colored pencils to draw the head of a dragon rising from the bottom edge of a strip of construction paper. Put a dot of felt-tip marker ink or mixed food colorings in the dragon's open mouth. Set the strip in a jar filled with about a half inch of water. Watch as the dragon's fiery breath appears.

Rainbow Pie

Cut a circle from the coffee filter. Draw a design using felt-tip markers. Fold the circle in half several times. Dip the tip in water. Watch the colors explode apart!

SCIENCE SPEAK

SUPER SEPARATION

Chromatography is the process used to separate the different substances of a mixture. Scientists use chromatography to separate particles from the air, so they can better understand the problem of air pollution. You just used it to separate the different pigments in dye.

Sparkling Star Dip

Making crystals is a beautiful way to remove the solute from the solution. Dip star-shaped pipe cleaners in the solution at night and by morning your stars will be sparkling!

What You Need

- **Jar**
- **Hot water**
- **Borax**
- **Tablespoon**
- **Pipe cleaners**
- **String**

What You Do

1 Ask a grownup to help you fill a jar with hot water (boiling water is best). Add borax, 1 tablespoon (15 ml) at a time until no more will dissolve. [This will be about 3 tablespoons (45 ml) per cup (250 ml) of hot water used.]

HOT! GET HELP!

2 Make a star shape with pipe cleaners, then attach a string to the shape. Place the star in the solution. Let it remain overnight.

3 The next morning, lift out the star by the string. Enjoy the sparkling results!

     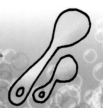 

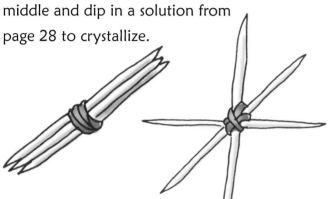

Six-Pointed Stars

Loop a small rubber band around a bundle of three toothpicks. Spread them apart for a star shape. Loop the band around each arm to hold the shape in place. Tie a string around the middle and dip in a solution from page 28 to crystallize.

Crystal Star Mobile

Punch holes about every 2½ inches (6 cm) around the rim of a yogurt container. Tie a 6-inch (15 cm) string from a hole. Add 2 inches (5 cm) to string length at each hole for a dramatic spiral effect. Attach crystallized stars to string ends. Hang the mobile from a string threaded through a hole in the bottom of the container.

MORE TO EXPLORE

- Repeat the experiment above using Epsom salts. (You'll need about twice as much Epsom salts as water.)
- Compare the shape of borax crystals with Epsom salts crystals.

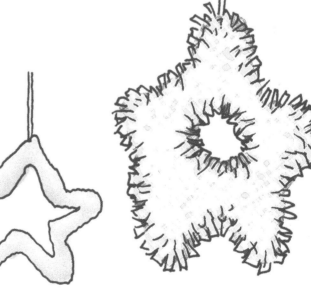

When you dissolve sugar in water, it seems to disappear. But is it really gone? Actually the sugar breaks down into tiny molecules that are impossible to see. Because hot water holds more sugar molecules than cold water, when the water cools and evaporates, it simply can't hold as much sugar. As water evaporates, sugar molecules come out of the water and stack together to form crystals. More crystals grow as more water evaporates.

SCIENCE SPEAK

When you dissolve a solid in a liquid, you make a solution. Growing crystals from a solution is easy. Just dissolve as much of a solid (like sugar) into a liquid (like water) as it can hold, until it is saturated (won't dissolve anymore). Next, let the liquid evaporate (see page 41) and solid crystals remain!

Solution. Dissolve solids, like sugar, in a liquid, like water.

Saturated solution. Dissolve as much of a solid as the liquid can hold, until solids start settling at the bottom.

Supersaturated solution. Heat the saturated solution and add even more solids. Cool it down. Supersaturated solutions are best for crystal-making.

Crystal Growing Tips

Don't rush. Crystals form best when the solution cools slowly.

Be patient. The more water that evaporates, the larger your crystals will grow.

Get a grownup. The hotter the water, the more solids will dissolve, and the sooner you'll have crystals.

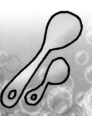

MORE FABULOUS FORMULAS

Make a variety of crystal solutions by supersaturating any of these solids in water. (Enjoy their beauty, but do not taste them!)

- Table salt
- Rock salt
- Sugar
- Baking soda
- Epsom salts
- Borax

Use your crystal solutions to make these projects:

Crystal clumps. Set the
jar of supersaturated water where it won't be disturbed and watch crystals form on the bottom and sides.

Crystal sculpture.
Set a pipe cleaner shape in the jar and watch crystals grow on the shape.

Science Clues
What happens if you heat sugar crystals? See Sugar Surprises!, page 32.

Crystal coats. Pour borax or
salt crystal solution in a pie pan. Fold thin cardboard (from a cracker box) in half. Cut out an animal shape so that the back of the animal is along the fold. Stand it up in the pan, and pour solution over the animal. Add more solution as it evaporates. How does your animal change over the next few days?

Geodes. Place small pieces of waxed paper
in sections of egg cartons. Set clean eggshell halves in the egg carton. Pour a small amount of crystal solution into the shell. In a few days, crystals will form inside the shell. It looks like a geode!

WHAT ON EARTH?

Gorgeous Geodes
Geodes are spheres of limestone. These ugly ducklings of the rock world contain a wonderful surprise. They're dull and ordinary on the outside, but dazzling on the inside. Crack them open to find quartz crystals growing within their hollow centers!

SUGAR SURPRISES!

Crystal Float Paperweight

Sparkling crystals appear suspended (floating) in this mysterious gel. The crystal solution is very hot so you'll need a grownup to help you prepare it.

1 Add a packet of unflavored gelatin to 1 cup (250 ml) of water in a pot. Heat to just boiling, then turn off the heat. Stir to dissolve the gelatin. Stir in sugar, ½ cup (125 ml) at a time until no more will dissolve—about 2½ cups (625 ml).

2 Pour the clear liquid into a glass jar leaving undissolved sugar at the bottom of the pot. Secure the lid.

3 Cool slowly by keeping the jar wrapped in a towel until cool. Place crystals where they will not be disturbed and you can observe their growth. It may take weeks for these crystals to appear, but it's well worth the wait.

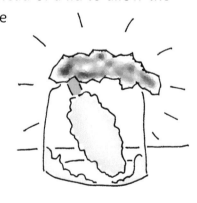

Razzle Dazzle Sticks

Follow the first two steps in Crystal Float Paperweight, but leave out the gelatin. Place ice-cream sticks in the jar. Use foil instead of a lid to allow the water to evaporate while keeping out dust. Leave undisturbed until crystals form on the sticks. You just made rock candy!

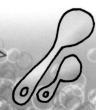

Can't Wait Crystals

Crystals usually take a long time to form, but here are some ways to make them appear quickly. Use the different crystal concoctions found on page 31 to make this crystal art.

Crystal frost. Use a cotton ball or small cloth to wipe crystal solution across a window. Wipe in only one direction. Wait about half an hour to see crystals appear!

Crystal paint. Use a separate, clean brush or cotton swab with each crystal solution. Paint a design or write your name on dark construction paper. Let it dry for a sparkling effect.

Crystal light-catchers. Pour a small amount of crystal solution into a jar or yogurt lid. Let the water evaporate. Crystals! Punch a hole at one edge to hang with string.

Almost-instant dips. Make a supersaturated solution of baking soda. (Alum, which is in the spice section of grocery stores or at pharmacies, also works.) Your pipe cleaner shape is crystallized in about half an hour!

Crystals Everywhere!

Watch snowflakes falling. You're seeing crystals in the sky. Sprinkle sugar on your cereal. You're eating them. Make a sand castle. You're building with them.

When the molecules or atoms of a substance line up in an organized, repeating pattern, that substance is a crystal. Different conditions can cause crystals to grow, but they always grow in regular, flat-sided shapes. A diamond is a valuable crystal that grows from heat and pressure beneath the earth's surface. By using evaporation you can grow rock candy, a delicious crystal, right on your kitchen table!

Make a model. Look at the different crystals you've made through a magnifying glass. They're a variety of shapes. Clusters of molecules join together in the six basic shapes shown on this page. Make a model of your favorite crystal shape using soda straws and paper clips as shown for Bubble Frames on page 116.

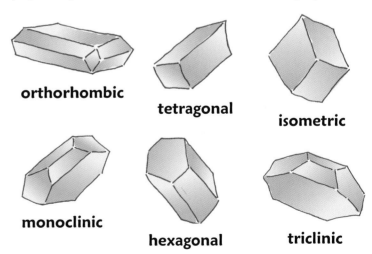

orthorhombic

tetragonal

isometric

monoclinic

hexagonal

triclinic

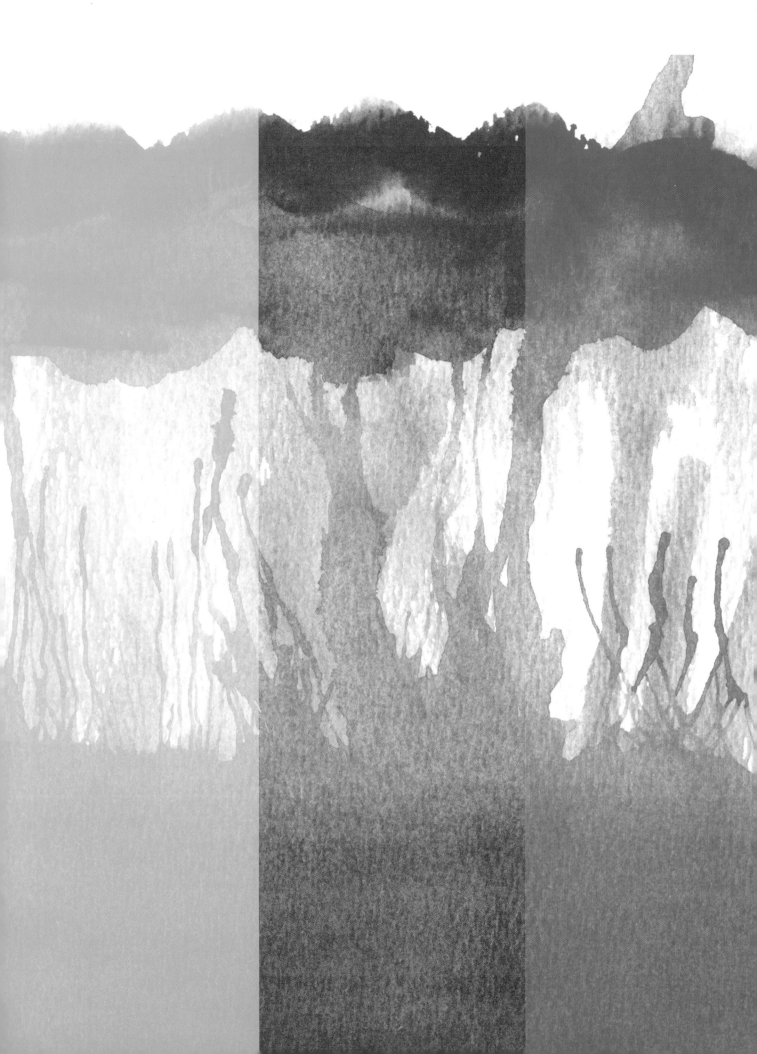

JUST a Phase

Amazing changes are happening all around you! Sometimes substances simply change from one form to another. We call this a *phase change*, or *physical change*, because the chemical makeup of the substance itself does not change. For example, a melting Popsicle changes form from a solid to a liquid puddle, but you could put the puddle in a freezer and presto—you have a Popsicle again. Eventually all that's left of the puddle, of course, is a sticky spot after the water has vaporized (another phase change) into the air.

Other times, substances change so completely, you can't recognize them any longer! These *chemical changes* happen when the atoms (see page 15) that make up substances combine in a completely new way. To make some amazing chemical change concoctions, see pages 51 to 67.

The concoctions here put phase changes to work for you. Investigate these changes right in your kitchen laboratory.

Frozen, Fried . . . Vaporized!

From a grain of sand to the planet Mars, from a raindrop to your dog's breath, all substances of the universe are made of matter in one of its three phases, or forms: solid, liquid, or gas. Make this concoction and you'll see water transform through all three phases. Can you guess the secret ingredient that makes it all happen?

What You Need
- **Ice cubes**
- **Frying pan**
- **Stove**

What You Do

1 Place ice cubes in a frying pan. Ask a grownup to turn on the heat and then watch the ice melt.

HOT! GET HELP!

2 The pan is now filled with water. Turn up the heat and watch the water boil. Notice the steaming water droplets rising into the air. Be careful—steam can burn you.

3 Turn off the heat when the pan is empty. The room is now filled with water vapor, an invisible gas, concocted from ice cubes!

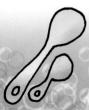

SoLid, Liquid, Gas

Scientists organize all matter (every possible substance) into three forms, or phases: solids, liquids, and gases. *Solids*, like rockets, pencils, and icebergs, are rigid and hold their shape. *Liquids*, like water and olive oil, slosh and flow and take the shape of their containers. *Gases* are difficult to sense, but we know they're there. Just think about how a limp balloon changes when it's filled with air.

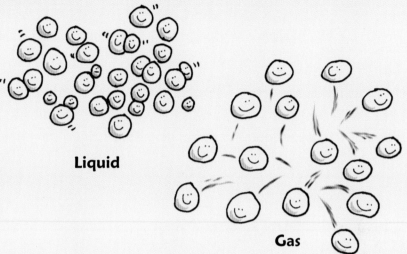

Solid

Liquid

Gas

MORE TO EXPLORE

Place an ice cube in a resealable plastic sandwich bag on a microwave-safe dish. Zap for about one minute and check. Continue to heat for 30-second zaps until the ice cubes have changed to liquid. Zap for another 30 seconds or until the bag is puffy. Why the puff? Because the bag is now filled with water vapor. The far-apart water molecules of a vapor take up more space than the tightly packed water molecules of an ice cube so they puff up the bag. Solid, liquid, gas—they're all in the bag!

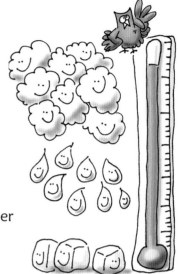

If a grownup has ever said, "You're just going through a phase," then you've got a lot in common with matter. Matter can change from one phase (form) to another by just adding or subtracting energy. To make ice, take away energy from liquid water. The cooled molecules slow down, move close together, and become solid ice. To melt the ice cube, add heat energy. The molecules move faster, spread apart, and solid ice changes to water. Add more heat energy to the water and the molecules move even faster and farther apart, changing liquid water to water vapor, a gas. So what's the secret ingredient that causes water to make three phase changes? That's right, heat energy!

SUPER FUN! Exploding Corn

Pop some corn and you create an explosion.

There's a tiny bit of water trapped in that kernel's tough outer hull. Heat the kernel and the water makes a phase change to a gas. As those water molecules expand, pressure builds, the hull splits, and the fluffy starch within blows out.

WHAT ON EARTH? Now You See It, Now You Don't

Given the right conditions, water can be as rigid as an iceberg, as flowing as a creek, or as invisible as a vapor. But no matter what its physical form—solid, liquid, gas—water is still water, with the same chemical makeup: 2 atoms of hydrogen and 1 atom of oxygen (H_2O).

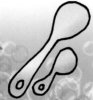

Evapu-Art!

Evaporating water can leave behind the prettiest puddle patterns. Hang puddle prints as ornaments in a window and let the sun shine through.

What You Need

- **Medicine dropper**
- **Watercolors (to make your own, see page 22)**
- **Plastic page protector**

What You Do

1 Use the dropper to drip watercolor puddles on the plastic.

2 When you like the puddle pattern, carefully set the plastic in the sun.

3 Keep checking on your art work. When the puddles dry, "puddle prints" of color will remain on the plastic.

SUPER FUN!

Suncatchers

Cut the colorful plastic into geometric shapes.

Punch a hole at one end of each shape. Thread with colorful string (see Capillary Colored String, page 100) and hang in the window.

Mix-ups

Add more puddles to the plastic after the first group has dried. Overlap some of the new puddles with the evaporated puddles. Drag puddle edges with a toothpick to create interesting shapes.

MORE TO EXPLORE

Compare Puddle Prints

Set one in the shade and one in the sun. Can you predict which puddle will evaporate first? What was the secret ingredient?

Make a Meltdown

Add different drops of food coloring to water in a few sections of an ice cube tray. Freeze. Then place colored, frozen cubes far from each other on a plastic page protector. Set in the sun and let the cube melt and then the water evaporate. How many phases of matter helped create your art?

Rainy Day Disappearing Act

WHAT ON EARTH?

It rained all morning and puddles are everywhere, but then the sun comes out and by the end of the day—no water! So where did it all go?

As an evaporation expert, you now know. Those water molecules at the puddles' surface bounced into the air and became water vapor.

You can keep track of the action with a piece of chalk. Make an outline of a puddle by drawing around the puddle's edge. (You don't have to wait for rain, just use a garden hose.) Draw new outlines every half hour. How long does it take for a puddle to evaporate on hot days? On cold days? In the shade? In the sun?

The Principle of the Thing

Water molecules are so active, they can escape from the surface at any time. When they escape, they change from liquid to gas, or water vapor, in a process called *evaporation*.

Evaporation happens at any temperature, but as you can see, your artwork evaporates more quickly in the sun (higher temperature) than in the shade. What kind of energy is at work here?

Did you notice that the flatter paint puddles disappeared first? That's because increasing water's surface area also speeds its evaporation. Now, can you explain why this is called Evapu-Art?

Out of Thin Air

When you cool down water vapor, the water molecules slow and move closer together, causing the vapor to liquefy into water droplets right out of the air!

ICE

What You Need
- **Jar with metal lid**
- **Hot tap water**
- **Ice cubes**

What You Do

1 Fill a jar with about an inch (2.5 cm) of hot tap water.

2 Flip the lid upside down and place on top of jar. Set ice cubes inside lid.

3 Now wait and observe. What do you notice on the underside of the lid? Where do those drops come from?

HOT TAP WATER

 **The Principle of the Thing**

Some of the water in the jar evaporates into water vapor. These gas molecules move quickly and some bang into the cold lid. The cooled water vapor molecules lose energy, slow down, and change to liquid (droplets) again. We call this process *condensation*.

SUPER FUN

Bathroom Art

Before your next shower, try this: Wet your finger, then rub it on a bar of soap. Use your soapy finger to draw a design or message on the bathroom mirror. Then, take your shower. How does the mirror look when you're finished? Where did the water on the mirror come from?

Why doesn't the water stick to the soapy spots? For a clue, see page 91.

WHAT ON EARTH?

Dusty Rain?

That's right! Dust is an ingredient of a raindrop. You see, clouds are made of water vapor and when that vapor condenses on dust particles, it forms water droplets. If enough of these droplets bump into each other and connect, they become heavy and fall to earth as raindrops.

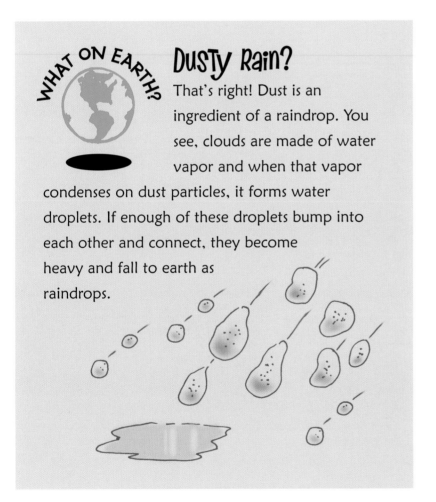

MORE TO EXPLORE

Cool Droplets

The next time you sip an icy drink on a warm day, observe your glass carefully. What's all that water doing on the outside of your glass? Cold air just can't hold as much water as warm air can. So, when your drink cools the warm air that surrounds it, the water in that air comes out—right on the cold surface of your glass!

Phase-Change Candle

Getting things to change phase just takes energy! Heat energy produces plenty of phase changes for paraffin and water. The result is a most unusual candle. Be sure a grownup helps you with this activity.

What You Need

- **Paraffin**
- **Coffee can**
- **Pot**
- **Water**
- **Stove**
- **Quart milk carton, cleaned thoroughly**
- **Candle as tall as the carton**
- **Crushed ice**

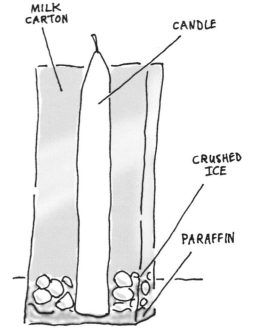

What You Do

1 See Safety First and Melting Paraffin on page 45 before melting the paraffin.

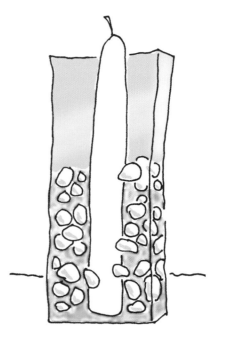

2 Ask a grownup to pour a dab of melted paraffin into the milk carton. Set the candle in the liquid, holding it until the paraffin hardens.

3 Once the candle is firmly in place, you add a handful of crushed ice. Ask a grownup to slowly pour more paraffin to cover the ice.

4 Repeat the layering in step 3 until the carton is full, but the candle's wick is still exposed. Let cool.

5 Pour the water from the cooled candle. How did the liquid form? Let the candle harden overnight.

6 Gently tear and peel the carton from the candle.

7 It looks like Swiss cheese, but it's a lovely and useful Phase-Change Candle.

SAFETY FIRST

Be sure a grownup is the only person to heat the paraffin and to handle the hot paraffin. The grownup must supervise the entire activity.

- Do not overheat paraffin. It can cause a fire.
- Only heat paraffin over water as described.
- Use pot holders to handle coffee can.
- Make sure no younger children are nearby when hot paraffin is being used.

MELTING PARAFFIN

For grownups only:

1 Place paraffin chunks in a coffee can. Set the can in a pan filled with about 3 inches (7.5 cm) of water.

2 Heat the pan and can. Stir and heat just until all paraffin chunks liquefy. Immediately turn off the heat and remove the can.

3 To color, add small bits of crayon stubs. Stir until evenly colored.

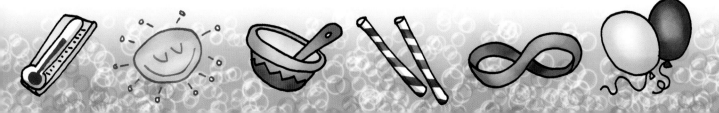

More phase changes than you can shake a wick at!

The paraffin is melted—solid to liquid.

The paraffin heats the ice—solid to liquid.

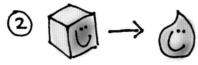

Some water evaporates—liquid to gas.

The ice and air temperature cool the paraffin—liquid to solid.

You light the candle and it melts—solid to liquid.

The paraffin near the wick vaporizes—liquid to gas.

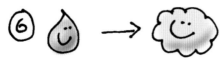

Water and paraffin can change phases. It's the addition or subtraction of heat energy that makes it happen.

MEXICAN-STYLE LANTERNS

Ask a grownup to pinch the cut edge of an empty can smooth with pliers. Fill can with water and freeze until solid. Set the can sideways on a towel. With the grownup's help, use a hammer and nail to punch out an interesting pattern around the top ¾ of the can. (Be careful not to let the nail slip sideways.) Set the can outside to melt the ice. Put a small votive candle at the bottom. Set the lantern in a pie tin. Turn down the lights and burn the candle for a lovely centerpiece.

NAIL
ICE
TOWEL

MORE TO EXPLORE

HOT! GET HELP!

Ask a grownup to drop spoonfuls of melted paraffin into a tub of cold water. Then you stir the water. Enjoy the strange, swirly shapes the paraffin takes.

A Day in the Life of a Molecule

If you were a molecule in a solid, you and your friends would be packed tightly together like bricks in a wall. That's why solids keep their shape, even when moved.

Too tight for comfort? Heat up a solid and the bonds between the molecules break up, causing it to melt into a liquid. Liquid molecules aren't so crowded. In fact, if you were a liquid molecule, you could wander where you pleased, but not too far from your friends. You'd be bumping into them all the time. That's why liquids flow and take the shape of their container.

If life in the fast lane suits you, perhaps you'd like to be a gas molecule! When a liquid heats up, molecules move so rapidly that they break away and become a gas. Life as a gas molecule might get lonely, because they are always on the move and stay far apart from each other.

Dance of The Phase Changes

SUPER FUN

You and your friends are molecules of matter changing phase. First cluster together making your bodies any shape you please. Hold still. You're a rigid solid. Now make flowing movements as you become a sloshy liquid while still staying close to your friends. Next, dart all around the room, moving further apart from each other, behaving like gas molecules. Can you find music to match the mood of each phase?

SOLID

LIQUID

GAS

Chocolate Meltdown

Phase changes are not only amazing, they can be delicious too! Invite a grownup to help with the heating and eating of this one.

What You Need

- **½ cup (125 ml) chocolate chips**
- **Double boiler or microwave-safe dish**
- **Waxed paper**

What You Do

1 Place the chips in a dish. Microwave on high for one minute. Stir. Repeat for 30 seconds, or until chips are liquefied. Or stir as chips melt in the top section of a double boiler.

HOT! GET HELP!

2 Dribble spoonfuls of liquefied chocolate onto the waxed paper. (Press in raisins, nuts, or mini-marshmallows, if you like.) Let the dollops harden, or solidify, in the refrigerator.

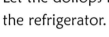
The Principle of the Thing

It's scrumptious science! Heating the chips adds energy to the chocolate molecules and gets them moving far enough apart to flow and become liquid. When you cool them down in the refrigerator, the molecules come closer together again to form a delicious solid.

MORE TO EXPLORE

Chocolate Spoons

Dip heat-proof plastic spoons into melted chocolate. Set on waxed paper and refrigerate to harden. Tie a bow around the handle. You've made a gourmet gift—a stirring spoon for coffee or cocoa lovers. What sort of phase change will occur when the spoons are used as stirrers in hot drinks?

Chocolate Bowls

Wrap small apples in plastic sandwich bags and secure with twist ties. Dip halfway into the chocolate; let excess run off. Set upside down on waxed paper in the refrigerator for several hours. Carefully remove apple and plastic from the chocolate. Fill chocolate bowls with sliced fruit, whipped cream, or ice cream.

Frozen Hands

Partially fill a disposable plastic glove with water. Secure the end with a twist tie and freeze. After several hours, cut away the glove. What weird shape is the water now? Why?

SUPER FUN! Here are four delicious ways to solidify melted chocolate:

Swirls. In a bowl, swirl liquified chocolate into ¼ cup (50 ml) peanut butter. Drop spoonfuls onto waxed paper. Add dollops of peanut butter to the center. Freeze to solid phase.

Fondue. Refrigerate dry strawberries, walnut halves, and seedless orange sections. Hold pieces by stem or tip; dip halfway into liquid chocolate. Set on tray covered with waxed paper. Refrigerate until chocolate solidifies.

Sundae. Add ¼ cup (50 ml) water when heating chips. Dribble liquid chocolate mixture over ice cream. What phase change does the chocolate undergo as it hits the frozen surface? What phase change does the ice cream make when it's hit by the hot chocolate?

Banana pops. Cut a peeled banana in half; insert an ice-cream stick through the cut end. Then, freeze. Dip frozen banana pops in the liquified chocolate; then roll in crushed peanuts. Keep frozen until ready to eat.

presTo Change-o

In Just a Phase (pages 35–49), you saw phase changes happening just about everywhere! Remember phase changes, or physical changes, happen when a substance changes from one form (like a liquid) to another (like a solid) and even back again!

Other times, substances can change so completely, you can't recognize them any longer. These chemical changes happen when the atoms (see page 15) have been completely rearranged to create a product with molecules totally different from the old. When you bake a cake, for example, the finished cake is very different from the flour, sugar, eggs, and water from which it was made. They've combined to create something wonderfully new and different. It all happens because of chemical change!

Get ready for some science surprises as chemical changes happen right before your eyes!

Lava!

Baking soda and vinegar combine to make an amazing substance—gas! Just add dishwashing liquid and you've got a bubbly foam that looks like lava. It's a great introduction to the world of chemical changes too!

What You Need

- **Damp sand or dirt**
- **Can (one end removed)**
- **¼ cup (50 ml) baking soda**
- **Pitcher**
- **½ cup (125 ml) water**
- **½ cup (125 ml) vinegar**
- **¼ cup (50 ml) dishwashing liquid**
- **Red food coloring**

What You Do

1 Mound up dirt or sand in your yard to make a volcano shape. Or work inside using a tray of sand.

2 Press a can into the top. Leaving the top uncovered, build up the sand around the can until it is hidden.

3 Place the baking soda in the can. Mix water, vinegar, dishwashing liquid, and food coloring in a pitcher.

4 Ready for the eruption? Pour the vinegar mixture into the can and watch the "lava" flow!

The Principle of the Thing

Substances often meet without much change occurring. When you add a spoonful of baking soda to a few spoonfuls of water, you end up with a solution (see page 17) of cloudy water.

But what happens when you add a spoonful of baking soda to a few spoonfuls of vinegar? Just watch it fizz! You've created a completely new substance called *carbon dioxide gas*; it is totally different from the vinegar or baking soda you started with. The atoms have been completely rearranged to create a product with molecules totally different from the old. When an entirely new and different substance is created, that meeting is called a *chemical reaction*.

SUPER FUN

Concoct a Dancing Drink

Add a small handful of raisins to a glass of fresh, bubbly soda and watch the action. Why do they dance? Because bubbles like to stick on surfaces. Soda pop is filled with carbon dioxide bubbles that cling to the raisins and lift them to the surface. When the bubbles burst, the raisins sink to the bottom. There, new bubbles collect on the raisins and the dance goes on!

LET'S GET PRACTICAL

Carbon Dioxide Was Here

Next time you eat a slice of cake look carefully at its texture. You'll see evidence that thousands of tiny carbon dioxide bubbles once were there. Cooks use chemical reactions to prepare light, luscious cakes.

MORE TO EXPLORE

You can use your kitchen-made carbon dioxide gas to actually power a boat! Make one from a plastic soda bottle with a tight-fitting cap.

CAP

BAKING SODA IN TISSUE PAPER PACKET

VINEGAR

STRAW

MODELING CLAY SEAL

1 Ask a grownup to poke a small hole near the bottom edge of the bottle. Insert a straw, leaving about 1 inch (2.5 cm) hanging out. Use modeling clay to seal the area around the straw.

2 Pour about a tablespoon (15 ml) of baking soda onto a 4-inch (10 cm) square of tissue paper or paper towel. Roll it up and twist both ends so it looks like a party favor. (Be sure this baking soda packet is narrow enough to slide into the bottle's mouth.)

3 Pour about ¼ cup (50 ml) vinegar into the top of the bottle, tilting the bottle so the vinegar doesn't leak out the straw.

4 Ready for the launch? Slip the packet into the bottle and quickly twist on the bottle cap. Set the boat in a tub of water and watch it go!

Hot Shapes

Create heat and a solid block of plaster from a mysterious mixture of powder and water. It's a chemical reaction that makes it all possible!

What You Need

- **1 cup (250 ml) plaster of Paris**
- **½ cup (125 ml) water**
- **Old bowl or large yogurt container**
- **Plastic bag**
- **Twist tie**

1 Mix the plaster of Paris and water in a bowl. Pour the mixture into a plastic bag and mold it into an interesting shape by pressing on the bag. Tie the end.

2 After about 10–20 minutes, feel the bag. Is it warm or cool?

3 Once the plaster hardens (about half an hour), remove it from the bag.

Warning: Never pour plaster of Paris down the drain, even when wet. It will harden and could destroy your plumbing. Dump leftover plaster in the trash.

The atoms in the plaster and water rearrange creating a product with completely different molecules to make a new substance. This process releases energy, in this case, heat, which explains why the plaster felt warm.

But did the plaster simply dry through evaporation to become hard? Not at all. Try this experiment to see for yourself:

Mix ½ cup (125 ml) of plaster and ¼ cup (50 ml) of water in an old container. Now pour 1 cup (250 ml) of water on top of the mixture. Wait about an hour; then pour off the water. Amazing! The plaster became hard as a rock, even underwater!

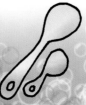

MORE TO EXPLORE

Hot Sculpture

Use this formula in step 1 (see page 55) to make a shape to carve: 1½ cups (375 ml) powdered vermiculite (from a garden center or nursery), 1 cup (250 ml) plaster of Paris, 1 cup (250 ml) water. Carve the hardened plaster with a spoon, creating anything you'd like. Use a nail for etching in details.

(see page 55)

LET'S GET PRACTICAL

Hard as Cement

Did you ever wonder how concrete bridge supports are made beneath lakes or the sea? Just like plaster of Paris, concrete hardens underwater. The concrete doesn't dry out; it goes through a chemical reaction called curing.

SUPER FUN! Look for animal prints in mud or sand. If you can't find any, use your own hand or foot to make prints. Make "alien" prints by pressing your fist, the side of your hand, or fingertips into the mud in strange ways.

Now make a cast of the prints. Mix twice as much plaster as water in an empty quart yogurt container. Pour a small puddle of the mixture on top of the tracks. Allow to dry, then lift off and rinse.

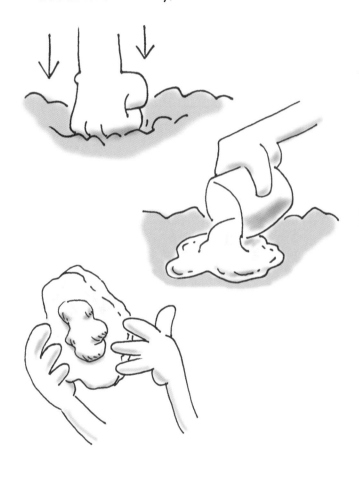

Blue Brew

Concoct a bluish brew that causes beautifully colored chemical reactions. We call this special brew an indicator because its color-changing reaction indicates (tells) something about the substance it comes in contact with.

What You Need

- **Red cabbage**
- **Knife (for a grownup's use only)**
- **Saucepan**
- **Distilled water**
- **Sieve**
- **Spouted measuring cup**
- **Spoon**
- **Storage jar with a lid**
- **3 clear film canisters or small jars**
- **Vinegar**
- **Baking soda**

What You Do

1 Chop up or shred the cabbage into small pieces. Place them in a saucepan.

2 Add enough water to cover. Simmer for about 20 minutes.

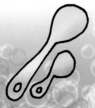

3 Let the brew cool for about half an hour.

4 Pour through a sieve and into a spouted measuring cup. Use the back of a spoon to push out all liquid from the cabbage; then pour into a storage jar. (Save the cabbage for Pickled Pink, page 64.)

5 Pour vinegar into the first canister. Mix ¼ teaspoon (1 ml) baking soda and ¼ teaspoon (1 ml) water in the next. Add tap water to the last.

6 Now add a spoonful of Blue Brew to each. Observe the colorful results.

SCIENCE SPEAK

Acids and bases are opposites. *Acids*, such as lemon juice or vinegar, are usually sour. *Bases*, such as soap or baking soda, are usually bitter. Many acids and bases are quite strong and can be poisonous, so tasting substances is not a safe way to determine if a substance is acid or base. Instead, scientists use color-changing *indicators* to determine acid and base.

Your face is an indicator, too. If you smile, it indicates that you're happy; frowning indicates you're sad or angry. Likewise, chemicals in red cabbage leaves can indicate if a substance is acid or base. Indicators help scientists better understand the makeup of a substance.

SCIENTIST-ON-THE-GO

How can you test foods without spilling Blue Brew in the pickle juice? Make handy indicator strips!

1 Cut a dozen or so strips of paper about 3" x ½" (7.5 cm x 1 cm). Submerge the strips in a pan of Blue Brew until fully soaked.

2 Use a fork to remove the strips. Place them on a plate in a warm place to dry.

3 Store dried strips in a resealable plastic bag. Dip a strip into any liquid you wish to test. Note the color change:

Pinks=acids

Greens=bases

**Blue (no change)
means the liquid is neutral.**

The Principle of the Thing

Mix an acid with another substance and you'll often get a chemical reaction. The same thing is true for a base. When acids and bases mix with indicators, the reaction produces a color change. Blue Brew turns pink in an acid, greenish in a base, and stays the same in a neutral (neither acid or base) substance. Scientists use these color-changing chemical reactions to identify acids and bases, and to gain valuable information about substances.

MORE TO EXPLORE

- Keep on dipping the indicator strips you made in Scientist-on-the-Go! Try testing lemonade, borax dissolved in water, fresh milk, sour milk, yogurt, antacid tablet dissolved in water, pineapple juice, toothpaste, sauerkraut juice, cream of tartar dissolved in water, catsup, egg white, milk of magnesia, saliva, and other liquids.

- Pass out indicator strips at a family meal. Let diners test foods on their plate.

Abraca-indicaTor

SUPER FUN !

Amaze your friends with a chemical reaction magic trick.

The mysterious blue liquid turns deep red when a clear liquid is added and back to its original color when a white powder is added.

1 Fill a tall glass with about ¼ cup (50 ml) Blue Brew (see page 58).

2 Hold up a glass of vinegar and say, "This clear, mysterious liquid will magically transform my Blue Brew into a Deep Red Brew. Abraca-science!" Now, you add just enough vinegar to make the color change— about ¼ cup (50 ml).

3 While your audience is still ohh-ing and ahh-ing, announce, "This magic white powder will turn the Deep Red Brew back to Blue Brew!" Now, you add just enough baking powder to reverse the color change—about ¼ teaspoon (1 ml). Presto! After some mysterious fizzing—it happens!

Can you explain the trick? Vinegar is an acid, so the brew turned pink. Baking soda is a base, the opposite of an acid. Adding a base to an acid neutralizes, or undoes, the effects of the acid. The Blue Brew is brought back to its original color and your audience thinks you're hot stuff!

LET'S GET PRACTICAL

Bee Acid

A bee sting contains an acid, while a wasp sting contains a base. Can you see why the folk remedy says to put baking soda on a bee sting and vinegar on a wasp sting?

SCIENCE SPEAK

An acid or a base can be made to be neither acid nor base. We call this process *neutralization*.

Magical Masterpiece

Imagine painting with "paints" that change color when they're brushed onto paper. It's not really magic; it's a chemical reaction!

What You Need

- **Blue Brew (see page 58)**
- **Pan**
- **White paper**
- **2 lids**
- **Vinegar**
- **Baking soda**
- **Water**
- **2 paintbrushes**

What You Do

1 Pour Blue Brew into a pan. Submerge sheets of paper in the brew and keep them there until they are colored.

2 Remove the sheets from the brew and set them in a warm place to dry.

3 Pour vinegar into one lid.

4 Mix water and a little baking soda in the other lid.

5 Using one brush for the vinegar and another for the baking soda mixture, brush the "paints" onto the paper. What magic colors appear?

VINEGAR

WATER AND BAKING SODA

MORE TO EXPLORE

Paint over acid brush strokes (pink) with bases and paint over base brush strokes (green) with acids. Can you neutralize the paint and bring the paper back to its original color?

The Principle of the Thing

Acids and bases produce color-changing chemical reactions when mixed with indicators. That's what you see in your painting. Acids and bases vary in strength, so their reactions vary in color.

MORE FABULOUS FORMULAS

Vinegar and lemon juice are both acids. Can you predict what will happen when you mix cabbage leaves or juice with these acids?

Pickled pink. Notice the color of the cabbage leaves leftover from making Blue Brew (page 58). Add a little vinegar and sugar to them. What color do they turn? Do you know why? These tangy pickles add color and flavor to any meal.

Blue cubes. Freeze Blue Brew in a few sections of an ice cube tray. Then, add the blue cubes to a glass of yellow lemonade. What color does the concoction become? Enjoy this mysterious, refreshing drink!

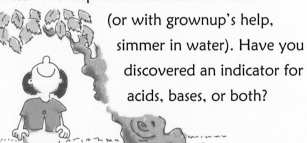

CURIOUS KIDS CAN Many plants contain color-changing chemicals. In fact, indicators may be found in leaves, petals, fruit, or other plant parts. Look for indicators lurking in canned or frozen berry juices and in juices such as pomegranate or cherry. Even red onion or peach skins and beet roots contain color-changing chemicals. Mash the suspected substance in water (or with grownup's help, simmer in water). Have you discovered an indicator for acids, bases, or both?

LET'S GET PRACTICAL

Dangerous Stuff

Some acids, like lemonade, you can drink—no problem. But stay away from sulfuric acid—it's so strong it can dissolve metal! You wash your hands with a base like soap, but you'd never want to touch caustic soda. It's a base that can burn and corrode. Remember: Never taste or touch when experimenting with unknown substances! Always wear goggles when experimenting with substances that might splash.

Acid Egg Bath

Give an egg an acid bath and you'll get an egg that can bounce!

What You Need
- **Hard-boiled egg**
- **Jar with lid**
- **Vinegar**

What You Do

1 Gently set the egg in a jar. Pour in enough vinegar to cover the egg.

2 Observe what forms on the shell.

3 Check the egg in about four hours and every hour thereafter.

4 Remove the egg when the shell is soft. Amaze your friends by bouncing the egg!

BOING!!

Egg Art

Use a crayon to write your name or draw a design on a hard-boiled egg. Gently set the egg in a jar of vinegar. Feel it every couple of hours to see if the crayon parts are slightly raised. If so, rinse the egg and gently wipe off the colored crayon. Your design will appear as a delicate raised pattern.

MORE TO EXPLORE

Place these items in a vinegar (acid) bath:

A raw egg. Check back the next morning. How has the egg changed?

A chicken bone. Check back after a few days. How does the bone feel?

A piece of limestone or chalk. Check out the bubbles that form. Does some of the chalk dissolve?

The Principle of the Thing

The carbon dioxide bubbles and soft, disappearing eggshell indicate a reaction between the two chemicals. Eggshells contain calcium carbonate (a base), while vinegar is made up of acetic acid. Crayon wax coats and protects the shell from the vinegar and thus keeps that part from reacting. This causes the protected areas of the egg to appear raised.

Vinegar also reacts with and dissolves the calcium carbonate found in bones and limestone (chalk). That's why you end up with a rubbery bone and bubbly chalk.

Vinegar Rain?

ECO-SCIENTIST

Not quite. But pollutants in the air do combine with moisture to form rain containing sulfuric, carbonic, and nitric acids. If you think this is bad news for our planet, you're right. While we may not be able to sense the difference, wildlife can. It doesn't take much acidity for rain to poison wildlife habitats like lakes and forests.

Acid rain's disastrous effects don't stop with nature. Some of the world's greatest monuments have deteriorated due to acid rain. Just as the calcium carbonate of egg shells reacts with vinegar, the calcium carbonate in limestone buildings and statues reacts with acid rain.

Indicator strips (see page 60) may not be sensitive enough to change color in something as mildly acidic as acid rain, but why not give it a try. Collect rainwater falling directly from the sky (not dripping from trees or buildings) in a clean jar. Test with an indicator strip. Test distilled water as well and compare your results.

Acid in Your Mouth

WHAT ON EARTH?

That weird slime covering your teeth in the morning is acid-producing bacteria. Your teeth are made of bone (just like the chicken bone). Acid (just like the vinegar bath) produced by bacteria dissolves the minerals in tooth enamel. So brush away the acid after each meal before it eats away at your tooth enamel and causes cavities!

The next time you lose a tooth, leave it in a jar of cola. How do you think the tooth will change? Observe it daily. Bet you'll never forget to brush your teeth again!

Go with The FLOW

The fact that liquids flow all over the place makes them terrific fun to explore. For example, honey, water, and oil are all liquids, so they all flow. But each flows in its own way. While water and oil readily spread out, honey will hardly budge. In this section, you can make concoctions that actually move and flow to help you compare these fascinating differences.

Liquids have other amazing properties. All liquids have weight, but equal amounts of different liquids don't necessarily have the same weight. And strange as it seems, not all liquids will mix together; they simply separate if you try. Knowing this, you'll discover how to make some incredible, layered liquid brews.

So let the fun flow as you slosh, pour, dribble, and stir wonderfully weird liquids.

SCIENCE SPEAK

Volume is the amount of space a substance fills.

Shape is the form a substance has.

GETTING IN SHAPE

How can you tell if a substance is a liquid? Just see if it flows to fill up its container! Put 1 cup (250 ml) of water to the test. Pour it into flat pans and tall bottles. How does its shape change? Now, remeasure. Does the amount of water change?

The water can take on any possible shape, but it still remains 1 cup (250 ml) of water. So, while liquids have a definite volume, they have no definite shape. This makes exploring liquids lots of fun!

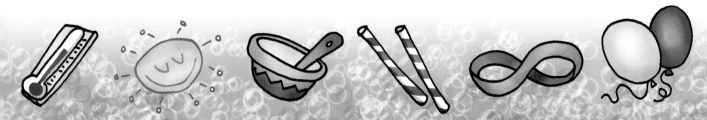

Viscosity Wands

Viscosity is all about how fast or slow liquids flow. Watch the dazzling display as you compare how water, rubbing alcohol, and cooking oil move.

What You Need

- **3 clear drinking straws (the jumbo size works best)**
- **Tall glass**
- **Water**
- **Tape**
- **Jar**
- **Tweezers**
- **Glitter**
- **Rubbing alcohol**
- **Cooking oil**

What You Do

1 Place a straw in a tall glass of water so that the straw becomes about ⅔ full.

2 Fold over a tiny edge of the straw's top and tape it tightly in place to seal.

3 Remove the straw and turn it upside down; then jiggle it so that the water flows into the sealed end. Carefully set the straw in an empty jar.

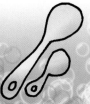

4 Use tweezers to add a pinch or two of glitter to the straw.

5 Repeat step 2 to seal the other end.

6 Now, repeat all steps using new straws and substituting alcohol and then oil for the water.

7 Tip your three wands in different directions, observing which liquid flows the fastest and which flows the slowest. Do any clog up?

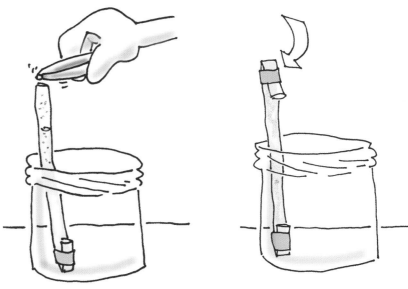

The Principle of the Thing

You know that all liquids take the shape of their containers. But without a container, liquids move out across the surface on which they are poured. Some liquids move with ease, like water. Others flow with difficulty, like honey. How readily liquids flow, or resist (hold back) flow, is called *viscosity*. As you tilt your wands, you can compare the viscosity of different liquids.

MORE TO EXPLORE GLITTER WANDS

Use a 40-inch (90 cm) length of ½-inch (1 cm) diameter clear, rigid aquarium tubing to make wands similar to store-bought wands. Use the whole length to make a super wand or have a grownup saw one tube into two or three wand sections. Pour liquids into the tube using a small funnel. Plug the ends with corks (available in hardware stores). Secure with a thin strip of duct tape, if necessary, or ask a grownup to seal the cork with a hot glue gun. Try some of these variations:

- Add food coloring, glitter, sequins, seed beads, or shreds of tinsel.
- Try using liquid soap or corn syrup.
- Add two liquids that won't mix (see page 84), such as oil and rubbing alcohol, to the same wand. How do they flow in the same space?

SCIENCE SPEAK Liquids flow in different ways. Liquids that hardly budge are considered *viscous*. Liquids that spread quickly and flow all over the place are *nonviscous*. A liquid's *viscosity* is determined by its "stickiness" or by how much it resists flow.

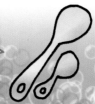

MORE FABULOUS FORMULAS

Flow-Motion Painting

Mix up paints of different viscosities for fascinating science art.

Fast-flow paint. Mix together 2 parts powdered tempera to 2 parts water. Stir until paint is evenly mixed and smooth.

Slow-flow paint. Blend 1 part each of flour, salt, and tempera powder to 1½ parts water until smooth.

Now try out your paints. Place a piece of paper in a tray. Drop spoonfuls of fast-flow and slow-flow paint onto the paper; then tilt the tray in different directions. Compare the paint paths and puddles each spoonful makes.

No-Flow Soup

SUPER FUN

Red and white soup side-by-side in the same bowl? Yes, tomato soup and cream of mushroom soup are so viscous, they barely flow into each other's space. Just follow the directions on the cans. Carefully ladle them side-by-side in an almost-flat bowl. Will they stay apart long enough for you to enjoy a colorful meal?

O.K. TO EAT!

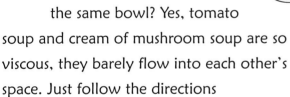

Move It!

It's a cold winter morning and the honey just won't pour out of the jar into your cereal. How can you make it less viscous and more fluid? Just heat it! Most liquids lose viscosity when they are heated. Their molecules move farther apart and presto, resistance is weakened. Ah, sweet cereal!

Hovering Veggies

What's that weird creature hovering between those two mysterious liquids?
It's a bird! It's a plane! It's a . . . carrot?

What You Need

- **Toothpicks**
- **Chunks and slices of potato, turnip, radish, carrot**
- **Raisins**
- **Cloves**
- **Jar**
- **Brine (see Concocting Brine, page 75)**
- **Water**
- **Food coloring**
- **Spoon**

What You Do

1 Create a veggie creature. For example, poke toothpicks tipped with raisins into the sides of a tube-shaped chunk of carrot. Use cloves for eyes.

2 Fill a jar half full with colored brine. Pour different-colored tap water down the back of a spoon to fill the jar.

3 Carefully set your creature into the concoction. Does it float on top, hover in the middle, or sink?

CONCOCTING BRINE

Half fill a bottle with hot tap water. Mark the water level with a line. See how many teaspoons of salt you can add without changing the level. Put on the lid and shake. Keep adding and shaking until no more salt will dissolve and you can see salt sinking to the bottom. Leave it for several hours until the water looks clear. Pour off the clear water into another bottle labeled "brine."

The Principle of the Thing

Notice how much salt you can add to water without changing the water's level. The amount of water stays the same, but by adding salt, you add more weight. If something stays the same size, but gets heavier, we say it's more *dense*. So which is more dense, tap water or brine?

Your creature sinks through the tap water because it's more dense than tap water. But it floats in brine because it's less dense than brine. Brine is so dense that even tap water can float on top of it. Not only did you make a vegetable hover, you found a way to make water float on top of itself!

TAP WATER MOLECULES

BRINE MOLECULES

MORE TO EXPLORE

What else will hover?

- Try small objects.
- Create more creatures.
- Try a hard-boiled egg or a slice of potato.

Remember, if it's more dense than tap water but less dense than brine, it will hover!

SCIENCE SPEAK

Density is the measurement of how heavy something is compared with its volume (see page 69). Weigh a box of feathers and then the same size box filled with sand.

They're both the same volume, but which one weighs more? That's right— the one with the higher density! And density applies not just to liquids; solids have density too.

CURIOUS KIDS CAN

A lump of clay sinks in water because it's more dense than the water. Remember, an object will float if it is less dense than the liquid. Density is the weight of something compared to its size. Can you get the clay to float by changing its shape to make it less dense? (Clue: The weight of the clay stays the same. Can you do something to increase its size?)

Science Clues

Where does the salt go? For a clue see 1 + 1 ≠ 2 Brew on page 23. Check the color of the concoction the next day. Why the change? For a clue, see Molecules in Motion on page 20.

 **SUPER FUN**

Brine Design

Brine is so dense that food coloring can float on its surface. Although the coloring will eventually mix with the brine, it floats on top long enough for you to capture a design.

1 Fill a pan with brine.

2 Cut pieces of newsprint smaller than the pan in any shape you like.

3 Drip food-coloring drops onto the brine. Swirl with a toothpick. Quickly and carefully place a sheet of paper on top of the coloring to pick up your design. When the paper is wet, lift it up. Lay flat to dry.

4 Try it again; then repeat with new colors.

Science Clues

How do the Brine Design colors get onto the paper? See Capillary Dip 'n' Dye, page 99.

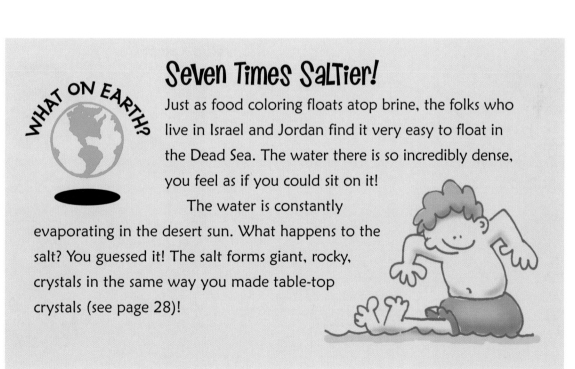

WHAT ON EARTH?

Seven Times Saltier!

Just as food coloring floats atop brine, the folks who live in Israel and Jordan find it very easy to float in the Dead Sea. The water there is so incredibly dense, you feel as if you could sit on it!

The water is constantly evaporating in the desert sun. What happens to the salt? You guessed it! The salt forms giant, rocky, crystals in the same way you made table-top crystals (see page 28)!

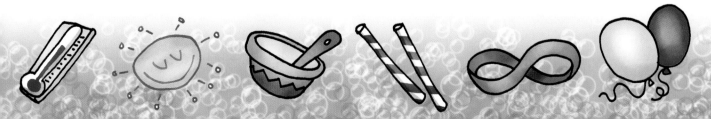

YeLLow+Red≠Orange Brew

When does yellow plus red not make orange? Amaze your friends with this tricky brew that just won't mix.

WhaT You Need
- **2 bottles or pitchers**
- **Water**
- **Tray**
- **Food coloring**
- **4 jars (all of the same size)**
- **2 index cards**

WhaT You Do

1 Place a pitcher of water in the refrigerator overnight. Right before the show, prepare a pitcher of hot tap water.

2 Concoct this brew over a tray to catch spills. Have your audience watch as you place a few drops of blue food coloring in one jar and a few drops of yellow in the other. Then, fill the blue jar with hot water and the yellow with cold water.

3 Ask your audience to predict the color if you mixed some of the yellow and blue together. (They'll guess green. Blue + Yellow = Green.)

4 Next, place an index card on top of the jar with yellow water. Now carefully invert it and set it on top of the jar with blue water.

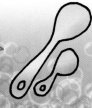

5 Slide out the card. Whoosh! The cold yellow water sinks and mixes with the blue. The audience is right—the concoction is green.

6 Repeat steps 2, 3, and 4, this time using yellow and red coloring, and quietly noticing which color jar contains the hot water. Again, ask your audience to guess the mixed color. (They'll guess orange. Red + Yellow = Orange.)

7 This time, be sure to place the hot water color on top of the cold water color. Say "Abraca-science!" as you slide out the card.

8 Incredible! The new concoction does not mix. The hot water color stays on top of the cold water color. Only a thin band of orange forms between the two colors.

The Principle of the Thing

Cold water molecules are fairly close together. But when you add heat to the water, the molecules move more quickly and farther apart. So which is denser, a cup of cold water or hot water? It's the cold water—the one that packs in the most water molecules!

In the first part of the trick, dense, cold water sinks beneath less dense warm water, and along the way, the two waters mix as expected. In the second part, less dense hot water floats "magically" above heavy, more dense cold water. What do you think will happen as the water temperatures even out?

CURIOUS KIDS CAN Can you think of a way to repeat this experiment using brine and tap water (see Hovering Veggies experiment, page 74)? Here's a clue: Are brine and tap water the same density? Which is heavier? How can you layer them to keep them from mixing?

Up, Up, and Away

Warm water is less dense than cool water. So is warm air less dense than cool air? See for yourself. Do this experiment on an open, concrete driveway on a calm, windless day. **You must have a grownup to help you do this experiment.**

1 Make several "air tubes." Fold a sheet of notebook paper in half to use as a pattern. Cut several rectangles the size of the pattern [about 8.5" (21 cm) x 5.5" (13.5 cm)] from tissue paper. Roll them lengthwise into tall tubes; use as little rubber cement as possible to hold them together.

2 Stand 1 tube in a metal pan. Stand back! Ask the grownup to light the top of the tube with a match.

3 The paper tube should burn down to an ash tube that "magically" rises high in the air. (If not, you've got extra tubes ready to try again.)

Why the rising column? Inside the ash tube is warm air. Warm air is less dense than cool air because its molecules are farther apart. So warm air rises. The ash tube is light enough to come along for the upward ride!

Two-Tone Tea

1 Using an orange, slice a circle from the widest part so that it fits crosswise and about halfway down in a drinking glass. Remove the orange and fill the glass to that level with refrigerated juice. Put the orange slice back in position so it sits wedged in the glass on top of the juice.

2 Ask a grownup to help you brew a cup of warm tea. Carefully pour it over the back of a spoon on top of the orange.

HOT! GET HELP!

3 Now, astonish a thirsty friend by gently pushing the orange slice vertically with a table knife so that the two liquids come in contact. "Magically" they still stay separate before your astonished guest. Add ice and enjoy.

Brown and White Cocoa

What's the mysterious ingredient that keeps these drinks apart? Temperature, of course!

1 Put 1 teaspoon (5 ml) of powdered cocoa and 2 teaspoons (10 ml) of sugar in a clear glass mug. Ask a grownup to add boiling water. Stir.

2 Slowly add a little cold milk or cream. Watch it whoosh to the bottom of the mug before it starts to spread out, or diffuse (see page 22). Watch what happens when grownups add cream to hot coffee. Can you explain what's happening? Eventually the temperatures will even out and the liquids will mix—without a spoon and your help!

WHAT ON EARTH?

When Cold and Warm Air Meet

What happens when a cold mass of air collides with a warm mass of air? Well, now you know that the two do not mix. Instead, the cold air pushes beneath the warm air. Water vapor condenses (see page 42) into clouds. Better get on your raincoat—showers are sure to follow!

Liquid Lasagna

What do you think will happen if you pour honey, water, and cooking oil into a jar? If you think you'll end up with a disgusting oily-watery-sweet mess, then prepare to be surprised!

What You Need

- **Measuring cup with a pouring edge**
- **½ cup (125 ml) honey, molasses, or syrup**
- **Clear glass or plastic pint jar**
- **½ cup (125 ml) water**
- **Spoon**
- **½ cup (125 ml) cooking oil**

What You Do

1 Pour the honey into the jar.

2 Now slowly pour the water on top of the honey. To slow down the flow, pour the water against the back side of a spoon. The water should float on top of the honey.

3 In the same way, trickle the oil on top of the water.

4 Check out the results. Why do you think this concoction is called Liquid Lasagna?

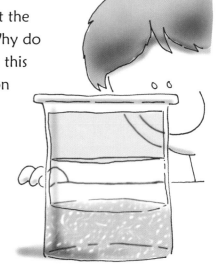

The Principle of the Thing

Liquid Lasagna shows that liquids have different densities. To compare liquid density, fill 3 small paper cups with exactly the same amount of honey, water, and vegetable oil, making them all have the same volume. Now compare their densities by weighing each cup on a postal scale. Which cup of liquid is the heaviest or most dense? Which is the lightest or least dense? Remember, each liquid takes up the same volume, but their weights vary. How do the densities of the liquids compare with their stacking order in the jar? Heavy honey on the bottom, oil on the top—aha!

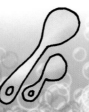

SUPER FUN! DENSITY NECKLACE

Create a lovely piece of wearable science art. Fill about 2 feet (60 cm) of ¼-inch (5 mm) clear, plastic tubing (available at hardware stores) with liquids of different densities. Ask a grownup to help with the tricky parts.

1 Make a tiny paper funnel for each liquid by taping a small sheet of paper into a cone shape. Pour colored corn syrup into the center of the tubing as your helper holds up both ends. Next, add different-colored water to each end; then cooking oil. Finally, add colored rubbing alcohol.

2 When the tubing is filled close to the brim at both ends, jam a single ¼-inch (5 mm) wood dowel (hardware store) into both ends to plug the tubing. Your helper needs to continue holding the tubing upright so you don't lose any liquid.

3 Wind a small piece of duct tape over the seam.

4 Wear the circle of layered liquids or, hang in a window for a colorful light-catcher. Store on a hook, corn syrup down.

MORE TO EXPLORE

Floating liquids. Try using liquid soap or detergent instead of honey, and rubbing alcohol instead of the oil. How do these new liquids stack up?

Colorful liquids. Add different food colorings to the water and the rubbing alcohol. Mix coloring into corn syrup and use for the first layer.

Floating solids. Create weird concoctions of liquid layers and solids of different densities. Seal with a lid and you've made a fascinating paperweight. Try floating these items on your liquid concoctions: bottle cap, paper clip, cork, plastic toy piece, button, twig, raisin, or berry. Can you find an object to float on top of each layer?

? CURIOUS KIDS CAN Can you think of a way to concoct a Liquid Lasagna with four layers? Five? More?

THEY JUST WON'T MIX . . . OR WILL THEY?

From the fat floating on top of your chicken soup to the disastrous oil spills covering miles of ocean, you'll find strange liquids that just don't mix. They are so chemically different, like oil and water, that they simply will not combine. The less dense liquid ends up floating on top of the denser liquid.

Scientists say these liquids are *immiscible*.

Even though rubbing alcohol is lighter than water, it won't float on top of water. The two liquids start combining the minute they meet. They form a solution (see page 17) because they are so chemically similar. Scientists say these liquids are *miscible*.

MISCIBLE OR IMMISCIBLE?

You know the water layer floats above the corn syrup layer in your density necklace because water is less dense than corn syrup. But notice how the edges between the corn syrup and the water layers in your necklace are fuzzy. What's happening? The two liquids are miscible liquids starting to mix. Eventually they will combine to form a solution that's more dense than water but less dense than corn syrup.

On the other hand, the edges of the oil layer are sharp. That's because oil and water, and oil and rubbing alcohol, are immiscible liquids. No mixing here.

So, liquids may stay apart because they are chemically different, or because they have different densities, or for both reasons!

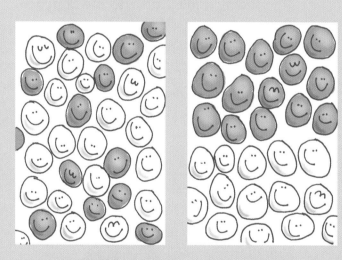

Miscible   Immiscible

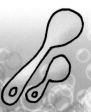

Mystery Marble

Add a drop of oil to a jar of water and rubbing alcohol, then observe what happens. The results are pretty enough to set on your windowsill!

What You Need

- **Clear jar with lid (jars with flat sides work best)**
- **Water**
- **Measuring cup with good pouring edge**
- **Food coloring**
- **Medicine-style dropper (available at drug stores)**
- **Cooking oil**
- **Rubbing alcohol**

What You Do

1 Fill the jar about ⅓ full of water. Add a drop or two of food coloring.

2 Use a medicine-style dropper to set an oil blob on top of the water.

3 Tilt the jar and gently trickle rubbing alcohol down the side.

4 Keep trickling rubbing alcohol until the blob forms a marble shape, floating in the middle of the mixture.

5 Seal with a lid so your masterpiece doesn't evaporate. Set on a windowsill to view.

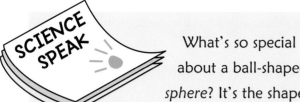
What's so special about a ball-shaped *sphere*? It's the shape with the least *surface area* (see page 106), the least amount of outside "skin." A sphere is also the shape a liquid takes when it's pushed with equal force from all directions.

Experiment with these changes, while creating a lovely set of light-catchers.

- Can you control the floating level of the marble by adding more or less water or alcohol?

- Use a medicine-style dropper to make different-sized oil marbles. Do they float at different levels?

- Use a pencil point to push stray oil droplets together.

The Principle of the Thing

You know from making Liquid Lasagna (page 82) that oil is lighter than water, but heavier than alcohol. So when you mix water and alcohol, you make a solution of just the right density to cause a drop of oil to hover.

At first the oil sits like a blob on top of the water because air pressure pushes it flat.

As you add alcohol, making the solution less dense, the blob sinks into the center of the water/alcohol solution. There it receives equal pushes from all directions, causing the oil to pull itself into a marble ball, or sphere.

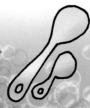

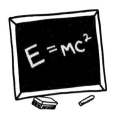

MORE FABULOUS FORMULAS

Use liquid density to create these super special effects:

Meltdown. Make a fascinating centerpiece for the dinner table. Will ice float on top of oil? What happens when it melts? Watch the action by placing an ice cube in a jar full of vegetable oil. Gigantic droplets of water form at the bottom of the cube. Where do they go? Why?

Ocean wave.

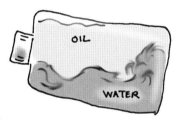

Purchase baby oil in a tall, flat plastic bottle. Remove half the oil and replace with blue-colored water. Secure the lid, hold the bottle on its side, and gently tilt it back and forth. You've created a model of ocean wave action!

LET'S GET PRACTICAL

Rolling Stone

From the time kids realized a small round stone could roll, they played marbles! In fact, archaeologists have found mysterious little

Fireworks. Fill a tall bottle almost full with water. Measure 1 tablespoon (15 ml) of cooking oil into a cup. Add a few drops of different food colorings; then beat well with a fork until the oil is speckled with tiny dabs of color. Pour the oil mixture onto the water in the bottle. Now, enjoy the fireworks display! Why do the dazzling streamers of color shoot downward, then eventually disappear? Here's a clue: food coloring is mostly water.

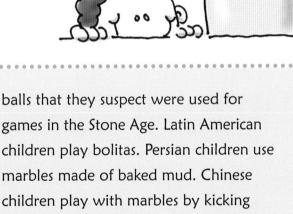

balls that they suspect were used for games in the Stone Age. Latin American children play bolitas. Persian children use marbles made of baked mud. Chinese children play with marbles by kicking them. The glass marbles we know are made by pressing melted glass between two half-sphere molds.

 **Delicious Density**

Ice water. Add an ice cube to a glass of water. Where does the ice end up? Why?

Root beer float. Add a scoop of ice cream to a glass of root beer. Where does the ice cream go? Why?

Peculiar Parfait

1 Blend 3 tablespoons (45 ml) of sugar with 8 ounces (228 ml) of cream cheese.

2 Ask a grownup to help you dissolve a package of orange gelatin dessert in 1 cup (250 ml) of boiling water. Gently stir in the cream cheese mixture.

**HOT!
GET HELP!**

3 Add 1 cup (250 ml) of cold water, a small drained can of mandarin orange sections, a handful each of mini-marshmallows and chocolate chips. Stir. Pour into 4 tall glasses and refrigerate until firm. Before you eat your orange parfait, notice where all the ingredients end up in the glass? Why?

 **Ducks Don't Get Wet**

The fact that oil and water don't mix (see Miscible or Immiscible?, page 84), is a big help to ducks and other water fowl. An oil gland near the duck's tail keeps water away from the duck's body, helping it to stay warm and afloat. The duck uses its bill to spread the oil over its feathers. Have you ever heard the expression "like water off a duck's back"? What do you think this means?

Oil Spill!

Petroleum oil spills are very destructive to wildlife. Oil floating on bodies of water coats swimming birds and other aquatic animals. A bird's feathers help it to fly and to stay warm; its fluffy feathers trap warm air and body heat the same way your puffy down jacket does. But when feathers are mashed down by sticky petroleum oil, birds can't stay warm; they die from lowered body temperature, or hypothermia.

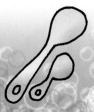

Get-IT-Together Mayonnaise

Can you force oil and water to stay together? Make a batch of this scientific spread and discover the secret ingredient that gets them to mix . . . well, sort of!

What You Need

- **Blender**
- **1 cup (250 ml) tofu (about ½ of a 14-ounce block)**
- **3 tablespoons (45 ml) vinegar**
- **Measuring cup**
- **½ cup (125 ml) olive oil**
- **Storage jar with lid**

What You Do

1 With a grownup's help, blend the tofu and 1 tablespoon (15 ml) of vinegar in a blender.

GET HELP!

2 With the blender running, slowly add the oil 1 drop at a time. After using about ⅓ of the oil, add another tablespoon (15 ml) of vinegar.

3 Repeat step 2 until you've used all the oil and vinegar and the concoction looks thick like mayonnaise. Do the oil and vinegar (made mostly of water) separate? What do you think holds them together?

4 For a gourmet treat, add a pinch of garlic powder, mustard, curry powder, or other spice to the spread. Or sweeten the mayonnaise with sugar or honey.

Note: This is tricky. Add oil one drop at a time. If your mayonnaise separates, use it for salad dressing and try again.

Oil and water don't mix, as you know. When you add an emulsifier to tiny drops of oil and vinegar, and then blend, the drops of oil won't touch each other and form a separate layer. In Get-It-Together Mayonnaise, the emulsifier is tofu. (In most mayonnaise recipes, egg yolk is the emulsifier.) Emulsifiers coat the tiny oil globs so they can be suspended (float, but not mix) throughout the vinegar.

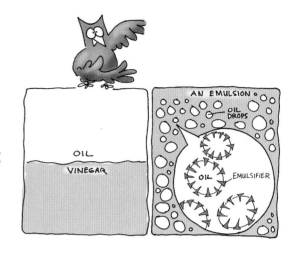

SCIENCE SPEAK

An *emulsifier* surrounds liquid droplets and keeps them from touching each other. It allows them to float in another liquid without separating. This new mixture of one immiscible liquid floating in another is called an *emulsion*.

MORE TO EXPLORE

Fill a jar half with water and half with oil; then shake. What happens? How do things look after a few minutes? In order to keep the oil mixed throughout the water, you must add an ingredient that will coat those oil droplets and keep them from sticking back together. A squirt of detergent does the trick. Repeat the experiment, using the detergent. Does the oil form a separate layer this time? (Does this remind you of an ad for dishwashing detergent?) You just made an oil and water emulsion with detergent as the emulsifier, coating the oil globs so they float throughout the water.

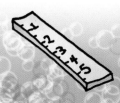

Push-IT-Apart Butter

What's the opposite of mayonnaise? It just may be butter. Mayonnaise-making brings fat (oil) and water (vinegar) together. Butter-making forces fat and water apart! If you shake cream with enough force, the tiny drops of fat that float throughout it are pushed together to form butter chunks. Find a friend to share in the shaking—and the eating—of homemade butter!

1 Fill a plastic jar about half full of cream. Add a clean marble. Seal with a lid.

2 Shake the jar vigorously in a figure-eight pattern. When you don't hear the clank of the marble any longer, you'll know the cream has thickened into whipped cream.

3 Keep shaking and listen again for the clank. This means the butter fat is separating from the liquid. When you see several small floating chunks, stop.

4 Use a fork to scoop the butter chunks into a bowl. Blend them together with the back of a spoon; then squeeze out the extra liquid. Spread the creamy butter on toast or muffins.

Science Clues

Why do the butter chunks float? See Liquid Lasagna, page 82 for a clue.

LET'S GET PRACTICAL

The Emulsion That Cleans

Get a first-hand feeling for how useful a soap emulsion can be. Rub a few drops of oil on your hand; then rinse it with water. Do you notice the water droplets clinging to the oil? The two liquids do not mix and the oil remains on your hand. Now rub in some soap and rinse. This time the soap surrounds the oil so it can float in the water—right off your hand and down the drain!

Sticky, creepy Water

It sticks to itself and to other stuff! It creeps in all directions! What is this weird substance? Would you believe it's simply water? Yes, water's unusual behavior makes it the perfect ingredient for some truly amazing science concoctions, so let the science fun flow!

Sticky stuff. If you don't believe how sticky water can be, try this: Pour some water on a slick surface, such as a kitchen countertop. Set a cookie sheet into the puddle, coating the bottom completely with water. Now, hang onto the rim of the cookie sheet and pull directly upward. It's not so easy, is it? That's because you're feeling the strength of water sticking to the cookie sheet and to the countertop. You're also feeling another amazing force—the water molecules sticking to each other.

Creepy, crawly liquid. For another science thrill, wipe up a grape juice spill using only a corner of a paper towel. Notice that most of the towel becomes a soggy, purple mess within seconds. Why? Water flows downhill, but on your towel it's creeping outward and upward. You've just discovered water's astonishing power to travel every which way!

Sticky Water

Is it possible to pour water from a pitcher into a glass 2 feet (60 cm) away? With the help of water's power to stick, you can amaze an audience with this incredible feat.

What You Need

- **Cup or pitcher with a handle and pouring spout**
- **Water**
- **Food coloring**
- **About 3 feet (90 cm) of string**
- **Drinking glass**

What You Do

1 Fill the pitcher half full of water. Add a few drops of food coloring for a dramatic effect.

2 Wet the string thoroughly. Tie one end to the pitcher handle and stretch it tightly across the spout. Let the other end fall into the glass.

3 With one hand, hold the pitcher by the handle about 1 foot (30 cm) above and 2 feet (60 cm) away from the glass, while the other hand holds the string against the inside of the glass.

4 Say "Abraca-Science" as you slowly pour the water down the string. It sticks to the string, magically making its way into the glass! Experiment to get the slope of the string just right.

The Principle of the Thing

The force of gravity, which pulls all things toward Earth, would like to pull water off the string and onto the ground. But two other forces are hard at work in this experiment. Adhesion keeps the water stuck to the string. Cohesion keeps the water stuck to itself. Together these forces keep the water flowing in a stream stuck to the string.

SCIENCE SPEAK

What makes water so sticky? When water molecules stick to each other, they create a force called *cohesion*. When water sticks to other substances, we call this *adhesion*. (Think: adhesion adds on.)

Remember:

Stick-to-itself force=cohesion
Stick-to-other-things force=adhesion

- What happens if you begin with dry string?
- Try the trick with soapy water. What happens?
- Find a friend, a ball of string, and head for the great outdoors. How far can you get the water to travel? You may have to stand on a step stool or at the top of a sloped hill to get just the right angle.
- Turn on the faucet so there's a slow flow of water. Insert a chopstick into the stream and slowly move the end of the chopstick in a circle. Can you make the water stream stick to the chopstick and follow in a circle?

SUPER FUN! Sticky Art

Water-based paint sticks to itself *(cohesion)* and also sticks to paper *(adhesion)*. Use these forces to create an unusual artistic design:

1 Fold a piece of paper in half; then open it. Spoon blobs of different-colored tempera paints along the centerfold. Then, add blobs anywhere else you like.

2 Refold the paper and use the palm of your hand to rub and push the paint from the centerfold outward.

3 Slowly open your painting. Can you feel the sticky bonds of the water-based paints? Notice the little ridges of paint on your picture—evidence of sticky forces trying to keep you from pulling the paper apart.

WHAT ON EARTH? Water!

You may have sipped the same water molecules that refreshed a triceratops millions of years ago! All water goes around in a cycle from rainfall, some used by plants and animals, to vapor through evaporation (see page 41). Vapor condenses (see page 42) to form clouds that produce rain, and the cycle continues.

Water is by far the most common and essential liquid on earth, covering much of the earth's surface. All forms of life depend upon it. Yet, with all that water, little is fit to drink.

Ocean water is too salty, and sadly people have seriously polluted not only oceans, but also fresh water rivers and lakes. Harmful liquids, like pesticides that seep into the ground, threaten *aquifers*, our great underground water sources.

The world's population continues to grow, and despite the fact that the amount of water remains constant, the amount of drinkable water is dwindling. Luckily, there are ways you can make a difference (see pages 106 and 110)!

Creepy Water Ghosts

Have you ever noticed how the whole towel gets wet when you blot up a spill? Water is creeping up into the tiny spaces between the cloth fibers. You can observe this amazing upward action by creating a thin space for water to climb.

What You Need

- **Jar lid**
- **Water**
- **Dark food coloring**
- **8½" x 11" (21 cm x 27.5 cm) plastic paper protector**
- **Scissors**
- **2 paper clips**
- **8"x 5" (20 cm x 12.5 cm) sheet of white paper**

What You Do

1 Fill the lid almost to the top with water. Add 10 drops of food coloring.

2 Cut the plastic protector in half so you have 2 plastic rectangles 8½" x 5½" (21 cm x 13.5 cm).

3 Place the plastic pieces on top of each other, roll them into a tube, and paper clip at both ends.

4 Stand the tube in the lid. For easier ghostly viewing, place a rolled sheet of white paper inside the plastic tube so it clings to the tube without touching the water.

5 Watch as watery ghosts creep between the sheets of plastic. The watery film is so thin that no matter how much coloring you add, it will appear ghostlike.

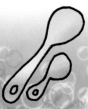

SCIENCE SPEAK

It's incredible! Water can defy gravity and travel upward. How does water accomplish this amazing feat? We know water would rather stick to certain surfaces than to itself (adhesion). With enough surface to adhere to, water can actually overcome gravity and pull itself upward. The conditions for this gravity-defying act are just right in a thin tube. With lots of surface to adhere to, water grabs onto the walls, raising itself long distances upward. We call this action, *capillary action*.

MORE TO EXPLORE

Insert a toothpick or long, thin stick between the plastic sheets. Does the water creep higher or flow back into the lid?

The Principle of the Thing

In general, water prefers to adhere (stick to other things) than to cohere (stick to itself). So when the water touches the plastic, it sticks and climbs up the wall. Why does water prefer to climb through tight spots? The narrower the passage, the more wall the water gets to adhere to, so the higher it rises.

Inserting the stick caused the water to flow out of the passage. There's just not enough adhering surface for all those water molecules.

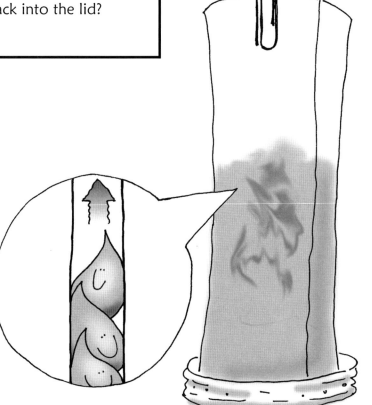

SUPER FUN SCIENCE SECRETS

Use capillary action to reveal secret science messages!

1 Create artistic shapes with parts that can be curled.

2 Use a waterproof pen to write secret science messages inside the part to be curled. Then, tightly curl around a pencil, hiding the message.

3 Gently set the paper on the water's surface, and observe the action.

Water just loves to fill the spaces between paper fibers. Once filled with water, the paper becomes stiff, forcing the curls to unroll and reveal your message.

LET'S GET PRACTICAL

A Day of Capillary Action

Q. What gets wetter the more it dries?
A. A towel!

Why? Because of capillary action. Dry yourself with a towel; let your breakfast cereal get soggy; mop up a spill; cook dry spaghetti; paint a watercolor picture; water a plant. It's almost impossible to spend the day without seeing capillary action at work. Draw a picture of a scene from your daily life. How many examples of capillary action can you show?

Capillary Dip 'n' Dye

Put capillary action to work to make science art. Absorbent papers such as coffee filters, paper towels, blotters, or rice paper work well for dip 'n' dye.

What You Need

- **Small bowls**
- **Water**
- **Food coloring**
- **Absorbent paper**

What You Do

1 Fill bowls about ¼ full of water.

2 Add different colors of food coloring to each bowl. The more you add, the more brilliant the colors.

3 Fold your paper as shown, or experiment with your own folds.

4 Dip the corners and edges of the folded paper into the bowls of different-colored dye. Watch the dye spread.

5 Unfold and let dry.

Paper is made of tiny fibers that form tiny tube-like spaces between each other. These spaces make perfect highways for water on the move. Water molecules on the top travel up these tubes by adhering to the paper. Water molecules down below cohere to each other so they're dragged along for the upward ride. The adhesive attraction of water for paper and the cohesive attraction of water for itself, are so strong they literally climb upwards. It's capillary action!

Capillary Colored String

SUPER FUN!

Add different colors of food coloring to small bowls of water. The more you add, the more brilliant the colors. Snake a length of wet string in and out of the bowls. Do not completely submerge your string so you can observe the colors creeping upward. Move the string, dipping new white parts into the dye. Let colors overlap. Let the string dry. Use to wrap gifts, to hang suncatchers or ornaments (see pages 29, 33, and 40), and to share with the birds for colorful nests!

SCIENCE SPEAK

Absorb comes from the Latin word *sorbere*, meaning to "suck up." Can you see why?

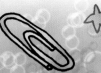

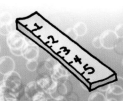

Can you think of a way to clean dirty water with a sock? Mix soil and water in a jar to make muddy water. Then, place the jar on top of a stack of books. Place an empty jar near the books. Now, using only a sock (and capillary action), how can you move the water from the top jar to the bottom jar, while leaving the dirt behind? For a clue, see page 94.

LET'S GET PRACTICAL

Nooks and Crannies

What makes a material absorbent? It's all those little holes for liquid to fill. A sponge is full of holes for water to fill, so a sponge is very absorbent. If you look at a coffee filter under a magnifying glass, you'll see more nooks and crannies among its fibers than you'll see on a piece of slick notebook paper. Which kind of paper do you think best absorbs color?

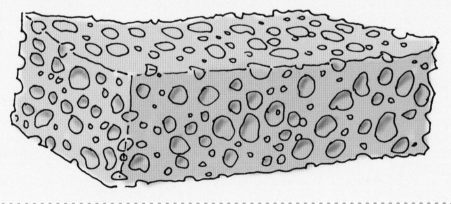

Penny Challenge

How many pennies can you slip into an already full glass of water? Take estimates from your friends; then experiment. Watch for a bulge at the surface of the water that will probably make those estimates all wet!

What You Need
- **Drinking glass**
- **Water**
- **Food coloring**
- **White paper**
- **About 30 pennies**

What You Do

1 Fill a glass to the top with water; then add a few drops of food coloring, and set the glass on white paper.

2 Add pennies, one at a time. Stop when water drips over the edge. Count the number of pennies you drop into the water and notice the strange bulge on the water's surface.

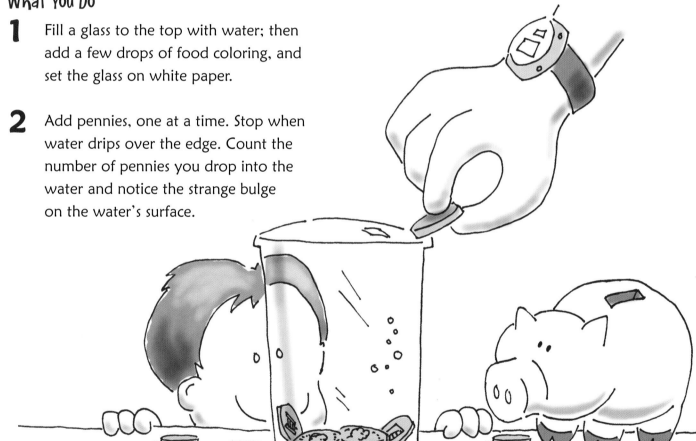

The Principle of the Thing

There's lots of sticking and pulling going on in your glass of water. Water molecules cling and tug on each other from all directions. But something special happens to the molecules right at the surface. With water molecules pulling at each other to the sides and from below, and with no water pulling from above, the molecules form a strong, stretchy skin across the water's surface. It's this attraction among molecules at the water's surface, called *surface tension*, that creates a skin tough enough to keep the water from overflowing—even when the water level gets higher than the walls of the glass!

But you can't keep adding pennies forever. They take up the space of the water molecules beneath the surface. Those water molecules push upward, breaking some of the bonds between the water molecules near the surface, and the water spills over the edge of the glass.

MORE TO EXPLORE

- Repeat the challenge, but this time add several squirts of liquid soap to the water. Does the glass hold more or fewer pennies? Does the bulge form on the water's surface?

- Place a penny on white paper. This time use a medicine-style dropper to place water on the penny's surface. Count how many drops the penny can hold. Does a bulge of water form on the penny?

SCIENCE SPEAK

Surface tension is a force so powerful that it causes a skin to form on the surface of water. It happens because water molecules are strongly attracted to and strongly pull at other water molecules from below and at the surface.

Science Clues

What simple ingredient found in every kitchen can conquer the force of surface tension? For a clue, see More to Explore on this page and page 112.

Spicy Art

Spices float calmly on a sea of surface tension. But what happens when you add soap? Capture a picture before and after; then compare the results.

What You Need

- **Bowl**
- **Water**
- **Paper**

You'll need a "palette" of salt-free spices:

- **Yellow: curry, turmeric**
- **Black: pepper**
- **Red: paprika**
- **Green: basil, tarragon, oregano**
- **Brown: cinnamon**

What You Do

1 Fill a bowl with water; then sprinkle the surface with a variety of herbs and spices.

2 Gently lay a sheet of paper over your spicy, floating design.

3 Place the sheet, spicy side up, in a warm place to dry.

Repeat steps 1 through 3, but this time add a squirt of liquid detergent after step 1. Compare these pictures with your soap-free versions. How are they different?

     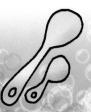 

No-Flow H₂O

A liquid that won't flow through a flimsy handkerchief?
What kind of strange substance is this, you ask?

What You Need
- **Pitcher**
- **Water**
- **Bottle**
- **Old handkerchief**
- **Rubber band**

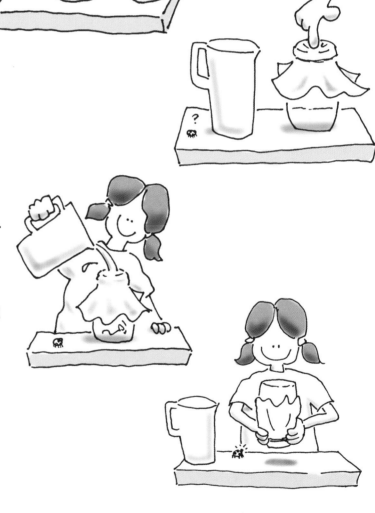

What You Do

1 Fill the pitcher with water. Cover the bottle with the handkerchief.

2 Push down on its center so that it dips into the bottle. Secure it in place with a rubber band.

3 Pour water from the pitcher into the bottle, through the handkerchief, showing your friends how easily it flows.

4 Say, "I can keep this magic liquid from flowing. Abraca-Science!" Then, tighten the cloth and hold onto the rubber band as you turn the bottle upside down. Your friends gasp expecting to see a puddle, but the water stays in the bottle without leaking through the cloth.

When you turn over the glass, the molecules across the bottom surface are pulled by other water molecules from above and to the sides. This pull, called *surface tension*, is so strong, it creates a tough water skin that spans the tiny holes between the cloth fibers and keeps the water from flowing through. It's surface tension to the rescue!

Keeping Dry with Something Wet

Umbrellas and tents work the same way to resist rain. The fine holes of the fabric are plugged with the surface tension of the raindrops. So when the fabric gets wet, it becomes water repellent and actually keeps you dry!

WATER WISE

ECO-SCIENTIST

Is a tiny leak wasting precious water in your home? Do a little math and see. Write down the number from your water meter before bedtime. In the morning, before anyone uses any water, check the meter and write down the numbers again. If the new number is larger, you have a leak! Check for leaky faucets indoors and out.

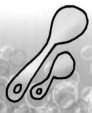

Poetry in Motion

Water is so wondrous, it deserves a poem. Write a "diamond poem" using this formula for each line:

Line 1: Water
Line 2: List two words that describe how water moves.
Line 3: List three words that describe how water looks.
Line 4: List two words that describe how water feels.
Line 5: Water.

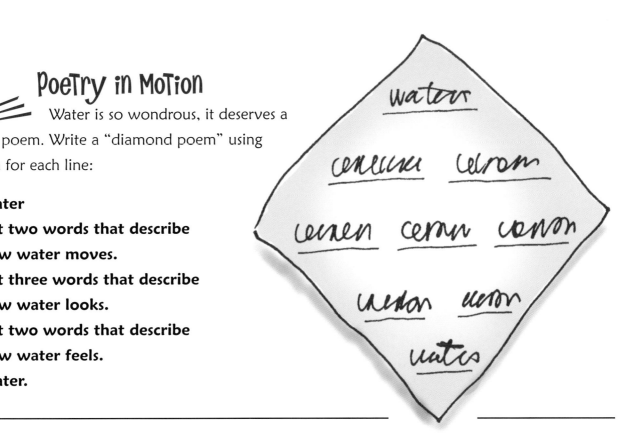

MORE TO EXPLORE A Hole in Water

Both alcohol and water have surface tension, but water's surface tension is stronger. So when alcohol's skin touches water's, the water pulls away, dragging the alcohol into a very thin film. This leaves what looks like a hole in the water. Say, "Bet I can put a hole in this puddle of water," and you've got another science magic trick to show off!

1 Pour a spoonful of colored water onto a plate.

2 Now add a few drops of rubbing alcohol to the center of the water.

3 Watch how the water pulls away, leaving a doughnut-shaped puddle. As the water pulls, it forms a ridge around the alcohol. Look closely and you'll see the ridge jiggle—water molecules tugging away, right before your eyes!

Water Ball Games

On your mark, get set, GO! Make a tiny water ball for yourself and a friend. Roll them across a miniature track and see whose water ball makes it to the finish line first . . . and in one piece!

What You Need

- **Water**
- **Film canisters**
- **Food coloring**
- **Ruler**
- **Waterproof marker**
- **Waxed paper**
- **Medicine-style dropper**
- **Drinking straws**

What You Do

1 For your water ball supply, place a spoonful of water in a film canister for each contestant. Add a couple of drops of coloring.

2 Using a ruler and a marker, draw two tracks about 10 inches (25 cm) long and about 3 inches (7.5 cm) apart on a sheet of waxed paper. Draw starting and finishing lines at either end.

3 Using the dropper, place same-size water ball droplets at the starting line, one for each player.

4 Now use straws to blow your balls to the finish line.

Note: If you blow too hard, you may blow your ball apart. If you do, go back and push your ball together again with your straw.

MORE TO EXPLORE

Drag it. Water adheres to other materials and coheres to itself, so try using a wet toothpick to pull your ball along. Set it on top of the drop and pull gently.

Bounce it. "Bounce" your ball forward by placing a wet cotton swab in front of your ball.

Solitaire. Cut a circle of waxed paper to fit inside a paper plate. Draw a spiral track that starts at the outer edge and winds its way to the center. Punch a hole or draw a spot in the very center to mark the finish line. By tilting the plate, see if you can guide your drop along the track. Too easy? Poke trap holes along the way.

Heap up. Splatter water on a sheet of waxed paper. Can you join all the small water balls into a single water heap by tilting the paper? Remember, water likes to cohere to itself.

The Principle of the Thing

Water molecules cling to each other so strongly that they pull a water drop into a ball. But if the drop is sitting on a surface, such as a sheet of paper, the water molecules also stick to the paper, flattening the drop into a blob. So which surface creates the better water ball, waterproof waxed paper or an absorbent paper towel?

Ball or Blob?

Drip drops of water on these different surfaces and compare their shapes:

- A glass plate
- A glass plate coated with detergent
- A glass plate coated with oil

What do you think makes the difference? Here's a clue: adhesive and cohesive forces are always both at work. The stronger the adhesive force, the more the water sticks to a surface and spreads out. When there's little adhesive force between water and a surface, cohesive forces are stronger. The water molecules within the drop pull on each other to form a ball.

So whether your drop looks like a ball or a blob depends on the constant fight between adhesive and cohesive forces.

WHAT ON EARTH?

Round as a Raindrop

After it rains, check out the water drops that linger on the waxy leaves of plants. They're almost perfect ball shapes. Water molecules within each drop tug tightly on each other— so tightly that the drop's outer surface acts like a skin that holds the drop in a ball shape.

Sticky, Creepy Water **109**

WATER DROPS ADD UP

ECO-SCIENTIST

Place a plastic 4-cup (1 l) measuring cup under a faucet. How long does it take to fill it? In only a few seconds, you've used a quart (liter) of water! Time how long it takes to do these tasks and you'll know how much water you can save by turning off the flow.

Brush your teeth. Do you turn off the water while you're brushing or let it flow?

Cool down. Do you drink refrigerated water or let it flow to cool?

Dishes. Do you use a rinse basin or flowing water?

Shower. How long do you take to shower?

Capture a Raindrop

SUPER FUN

Raindrop model. Mix two parts flour with one part salt. Fill a pan with about a half inch of this mixture. Carefully let water drip from your hand onto the flour and salt. (Better yet, on a rainy day, hold the pan outside for a few seconds.) Do not disturb for several hours. Then

use a fork to carefully lift out the wet spots of flour. Set them on a plate in a warm spot to dry. Compare the shapes of the raindrop models. Are they balls or blobs? Why?

Rainbow painting. Use tempera paints to paint a design. Set the dry painting outside for a minute on a rainy day. How do the raindrops change your design?

Tubful of Tension

Surface tension that is. Put everything you now know about this tough, invisible skin to use with the simplest of all concoctions—water!

What You Need

- **Plastic tub or baking pan**
- **Water**
- **Paper clips, pop-top rings, plastic tabs**
- **Paper**
- **Pencil**
- **Scissors**
- **Rubber cement**

What You Do

1 Fill the pan to about 1 inch (2.5 cm) from the top with water.

2 Hold a paper clip by one end and drop it into the water. It breaks through the skin of surface tension and sinks. Can you find a way to set the clip on the water's surface?

3 Now try to set other things on the water's tough skin. Pop-top rings, plastic tabs, and hair pins make great "surface-striding stuff." When you discover how to carefully place these items on top of the water, you're ready for the fun.

4 Think of the clips, rings, or tabs as feet, snowshoes, skates, or skis. Design paper creatures. Use rubber cement or tape to attach them as shown to the surface-striding stuff. Set them carefully on the water and observe.

MORE TO EXPLORE

Water robots. Cut your entire creature from aluminum foil. Fold the feet as shown and place on the water. What happens if you add a squirt of soap?

On the move. Use a straw to blow creatures across the tub from behind.

Magic loop. Knot thin string or thread into a loop; then set it on the water's surface. Squirt a drop of soap in the center of the string loop. It magically forms a circle.

Hole-y floater. Set a plastic berry basket on the water's surface. Can something so full of holes really float?

Zippy Boat Races

Cut a boat shape from an index card and decorate it with waterproof marking pens. Use rubber cement to attach a plastic tab at the back. Place a drop of liquid soap in the notch; then watch your boat zip across the tub. Try racing different boat designs with your friends.

Why does that soap squirt make the boat move? Soap weakens the pull of water molecules behind the boat while the pull at the front remains strong and pulls the boat forward.

Because soap weakens surface tension, the pan must be dumped and rinsed well after each race.

DROP OF SOAP

23

The Principle of the Thing

Water's tough skin supports your surface striders. But wherever you add soap, the pull of the water molecules is weakened and the skin breaks. Soap also weakens the surface tension at the center of the string loop, but the bonds on the other side of the string are still strong. Equal pull from all directions outside the loop causes the string to form a circle.

MiLky CoLor ExpLosions

*Create fantastic color explosions, not at a fireworks display,
but right in a plate of milk any day of the year!*

WhaT You Need

- **Plate**
- **Milk**
- **Food coloring**
- **Toothpick**
- **Liquid detergent**

WhaT You Do

1 Pour enough milk on the plate to coat the bottom completely.

2 When the milk is still, drip drops of different food colorings in the milk.

3 Dip a toothpick in liquid soap and place it in the middle of the color drops. Watch the drops of coloring explode and swirl.

WHAT ON EARTH? Water STriders Do IT

Ask a grownup to visit a pond with you. The water's surface is so still, you may be able to see your reflection. But if you take a careful look, you'll see a lot of action going on. Water striders everywhere! These funny bugs skate easily over the surface of the water thanks to surface tension. Special hairs on their legs and bodies allow them to barely dent the water's surface, without breaking through the water's tough skin. Middle legs paddle the striders wherever they want to go.

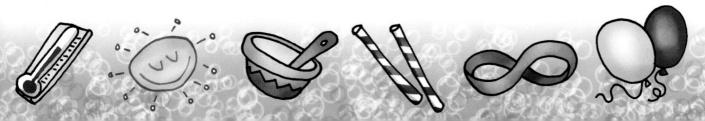

- Drip soap directly into the milk. What happens?

- Try different kinds of milk: 2%, non-fat, cream, half and half, evaporated. Which produces the best color patterns and movements?

The Principle of the Thing

One end of a detergent molecule is attracted to water and the other end is attracted to grease (fat). Milk contains both fat and water, so when you add detergent those soap molecules start grabbing onto their favorite parts of the milk. Food coloring is made mostly of water so it mixes with the water part of milk. All this molecular grabbing, moving, and mixing is what you see as explosions of color.

Mixed-Up Milk

Among other ingredients, milk is a mixture of fat and water, two immiscible liquids that don't ordinarily mix. The fat (cream) in milk naturally separates from the water and rises to the top. Today, however, milk is *homogenized*, a process that forces the cream through tiny holes. The cream droplets become so small they can float throughout the milk without coming together to form a layer at the top.

Science Clues

Why does cream rise to the top of non-homogenized milk? For a clue, see page 84.

Bubble Brew

Making bubbles means making water stretch, but tap water has too much surface tension to stretch. Discover the secret kitchen ingredient that reduces surface tension and allows water to stretch into a thin film that can surround a puff of air!

What You Need

- **Plastic bottle and cap**
- **4 cups (1 l) water**
- **½ cup (125 ml) liquid dish soap (Joy® or Dawn® works best)**
- **2 tablespoons (30 ml) sugar**

What You Do

1 Fill a bottle with the ingredients. Secure the cap and gently swish the brew back and forth to mix.

2 Let the brew settle and become froth-free. Now it's time to blow bubbles!

SUPER FUN! BLOWERS GaLore

A bubble blower is a frame that holds a soapy film. Blow air against the film and voila—a bubble! Compare the shape of the film before and after you blow. Experiment with all types of bubble blowers:

Your hand. Make a circle with your fingers.

A straw. Flatten one end and snip twice to create four fold-out flaps. Bend them so they form an X-shape. Dip this end. Blow through the other.

Monster maker. Thread string through two straws and tie the ends. Hold by the straws and dip. Wave in the air to release gigantic bubbles.

Square bubbles. Use bendable wire to form square or triangular-shaped frames. Do these frames change the spherical bubble shape?

3-D frames. Cut straws in half. Link two or three paper clips together to make connectors. Use them to join the straws into a cube (six squares form a cube) or tetrahedron (four triangles form a pyramid shape). Attach an extra clip at one corner to use as a holder. Although you might expect the soap film to cover the outside of these 3-D frames, it doesn't. Why do films form on the inside? Because there's less surface area, of course!

The Principle of the Thing

You can always guess the shape soap film will take—the shape with the least possible surface area (outside skin).

A bubble's beautiful sphere is the shape with the least surface area the soap film can take to surround a puff of air. So, even if you blow through a square frame, the bubble will always be round.

MORE TO EXPLORE

You Brew!

Bubble Brew is 1 part detergent to 8 parts water (see Discover the Relationship, page 122). But what happens if you add more or less parts water? More or less parts detergent? Change the amount of sugar? Or, instead of sugar, try adding a few teaspoons of glycerin, corn syrup, or gelatin. Keep track of the amounts of ingredients you use and note what you like or dislike about each brew.

Bubble Cubes

When you blow a bubble, it will always form a sphere. Is it possible, then, to transform a bubble from an ordinary sphere into an extraordinary cube?

Try this: Fill a soda bottle with Bubble Brew. Cover the opening with your hand as you turn the bottle upside down and let the brew slowly empty into the bowl. Turn the bottle right side up and observe. Is the bottle empty?

Packin' Them In

How many kids can you fit on a bench? Lots if everyone squeezes closely together and turns their bodies in just the right way. The same thing is true with bottled bubbles. The cube-like bubbles you see are bubbles trying to pack themselves into a tight space. Each bubble changes its shape to help make room for the rest.

Why all the bubbles? Because air is lighter than water, so it always stays on top of the Bubble Brew in the bottle. When you turn the bottle upside down, the air swooshes through the brew to make its way back on top. As it moves, it creates pockets of soapy film-covered air, or bubbles.

LET'S GET PRACTICAL

Fire-Fighting Bubbles

Why isn't water used to extinguish fires caused by burning oil? Since oil is lighter than water (see page 76), the oil floats on top of the water, continuing to burn. So what do firefighters do? They spray on a bubbly foam that cools and smothers what's burning without sinking through the oil like water. The light bubbles stay on top of the oil, keeping out the oxygen from the air that the fire needs. It's bubbles to the rescue!

Goo Globs of Fun

The world is full of stuff that's just plain weird! From mustard to mud, from slimy snail trails to raw eggs, from chewing gum to bouncing balls—strange-behaving goos and globs are everywhere! Explore your home and you'll discover plenty: lotion, glue, toothpaste, and even rubber bands to name just a few.

What makes these substances so weird? You'll discover the different reasons with each concoction you make. Some, like mud, float solid particles in a liquid. So these concoctions behave both like their solid particles and the liquid they float in. With other concoctions like gelatin, you can actually trap liquid molecules in a web of solid molecule chains. So these substances also behave something like a solid and something like a liquid. It's even possible to trap gas in a solid and produce foamy, yet solid-feeling stuff, like a marshmallow. And, you can make a chemical reaction that causes molecules to link up in a water-trapping pattern that feels like a rubbery gel.

Just follow the formulas in this section to create strange substances that don't behave like your typical solid, liquid, or gas. Experience the mucky, moldable, stretchy side of science!

Gooblek

Gooblek is weird stuff, for sure. But is it a solid or a liquid? Is it wet or dry? You decide!

What You Need
- ¾ **cup (175 ml) cornstarch**
- ½ **cup (125 ml) water**
- **Pan and spoon**

What You Do

1 Using a spoon, evenly blend the water with the cornstarch in a pan.

2 Gooblek should be thick enough to form a ball by rolling it between your palms. Add more water or cornstarch if needed.

3 Stick your hand in the concoction. How does Gooblek feel?

 MORE TO EXPLORE

Roll it. Roll Gooblek into a ball between your palms. What happens when you lift one hand away?

Break it. Can you break a chunk of Gooblek in half?

Slap it. Flatten the Gooblek in the pan; then slap it. Can you make the "liquid" splash?

Wet or dry? Touch the Gooblek in the pan. Then, squeeze some in your hand. Does it feel wet, dry, or both?

On or in? Set objects of different weights on the Gooblek. Do they stay on top or sink into the concoction?

Dry it. Place a pan of Gooblek in the sun for a few hours. What's left of the concoction? What happens when you add water?

Good-bye, Gooblek . . . Safely!

- Gooblek will clog drains. Do not pour it down the sink or flush it down the toilet.

- Dispose of Gooblek in the trash or throw in the compost bin.

- Let the water evaporate and you've got cornstarch again. Store dry granules in a resealable plastic bag. Just add water to reuse.

SCIENCE SPEAK

When you suspend (hang) particles of one substance in another substance, you create a *suspension*! The particles suspended in a liquid or a gas may be solid specks or liquid droplets. They will settle out over time. Amazingly, fog is a suspension of liquid water droplets in air, and smoke is a suspension of solid particles in air. Can you figure out what sort of suspension Gooblek creates?

The Principle of the Thing

You just suspended a solid (cornstarch) in a liquid (water), so the *suspension* you created acts like both a liquid and a solid. Mixing starch and water spaces the starch grains evenly throughout the water. When you move the Gooblek slowly, the grains have time to keep their even spacing and the Gooblek flows like a liquid.

When you move the Gooblek quickly (by squeezing, slapping, or rolling), the grains jam together and the Gooblek acts like a solid.

WATER CORNSTARCH — SLOWLY

QUICKLY

WATER CORNSTARCH

Concoct The Perfect Gooblek

Use a chart like the one to the right to keep track of your work. Start by mixing 3 spoonfuls of cornstarch with 2 spoonfuls of water. Too runny? Add another spoonful of cornstarch. Your chart should now read 4 to 2 (which, by the way, is the same as 2 to 1, or twice as much starch as water, or half as much water as starch!). Too thick? Add another spoonful of water. Now the proportion is 4 to 3. Add another spoonful of cornstarch, and you've got my favorite Gooblek concoction, 5 to 3. Hold your mixing spoon up high and marvel at the "solid" ribbons of Gooblek flowing back into the pan!

Cornstarch	Water	Proportion
3	2	3:2
4	2	2:1
4	3	4:3
5	3	5:3

Measure up a big batch. Once you discover your favorite mix, use paper cups or cans to measure out the perfect proportion of starch to water in a plastic tub outdoors. Invite your friends over for a backyard Gooblek bash. Hose down the mess when you're done. (Don't pour down the drain.)

DISCOVER THE RELATIONSHIP

The formula you just mixed is 3 parts of cornstarch and 2 parts of water. So we say the *proportion* (relationship) of cornstarch to water is 3 to 2. A part can be any size. You can use a coffee can or a tablespoon, just so long as you use the same device for all the measuring. When experimenting, it's best to use small amounts, like spoonfuls. That way you'll conserve materials and have better control of your results.

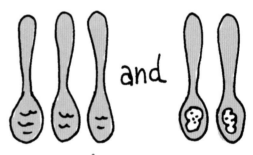

and

is the same relationship as:

and

GooblekLand

Imagine Gooblek covering the surface of a strange land. Can you create a creature or vehicle that can move across the land without sinking into it?

Set a fork in a pan of Gooblek and it sinks. Can you find objects that can rest on top without sinking? See Tub Full of Tension on page 111 for some ideas. Does the proportion of starch to water affect how you design your creature?

If a grownup lets you fill a kiddie pool with Gooblek (outdoors, please!), you're a lucky kid. You be the creature and start experimenting (keep a proportion chart). Try walking across it. Do you walk on it or in it?

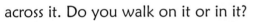

CORNSTARCH IS NONTOXIC

That means it's not poisonous. And it's safe to eat in food. Try these cornstarch tips:

Sticky swimming gear?
Dust fins, caps, and rafts at the end of swim season.

Sweaty tennies? Dust the insides of shoes.

Mud on the carpet? Sprinkle on, wait 15 minutes, and vacuum.

Science Clues

What makes a solid, solid? A liquid, liquid? A gas, gas? For a clue, see page 37.

WHAT ON EARTH? Maize, Zea, Corn

Scientists call it *Zea mays*. Native Americans call it *maize*. By any name, it's no wonder that corn is a treasured plant. Almost every part of it is useful. Enjoy the kernels right off the cob or grind them into cornmeal and use to make cereals, breads, tortillas, and hominy. Along with cornstarch, cooking oil also comes from the kernels of corn. Even the cobs are used to feed livestock. And what about those towering cornstalks? Millions of tons are made into paper, wallboard, and a rubber substitute called *maizolith*. Let corn ferment and you get a gas, *methyl alcohol*, that may be used to power automobiles someday.

Rashes, sunburn, poison ivy?
Add 1 cup (250 ml) to your bath water and soak. Use 4 tablespoons (50 ml) cornstarch to 3 tablespoons (40 ml) water for a soothing skin paste.

Dirty pots and pans? If you don't want to scratch them, sprinkle starch on your sponge and rub.

Goo Globs of Fun **123**

Jigglin' Gelatin Worms

Trap liquid juice inside a solid protein (see page 126) and you've got a jiggly substance called a colloid. These colloidal critters behave a little like a liquid, a little like a solid—and a lot like something good to eat!

What You Need

- **Unflavored gelatin**
- **Square cake pan**
- **Juice, boiling**
- **Spoon**
- **Drinking straws**
- **Jars**

What You Do

1 Pour one packet of unflavored gelatin into a cake pan; then ask a grownup to add ⅔ cup (150 ml) boiling juice. Stir until gelatin is dissolved. Cool until warm.

HOT! GET HELP!

2 Sink straws in the gelatin so that they fill up with the liquid. Place jars on top if they float. Refrigerate until firm (about 3 hours).

3 Place the chilled straws on a cutting board, and use a rolling pin, as shown, to push and roll the worms out of the straws. The longer you refrigerate the worms, the sturdier they become.

     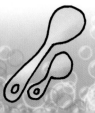 

MORE TO EXPLORE

HOT! GET HELP!

- What happens if you heat up a bowlful of gelatin worms? Will the liquid gel again if it chills? Use this discovery to make hardened Gela-glue reusable. (See More Fabulous Formulas on page 126.)

- It only takes a little gelatin to thicken a liquid. Change the amount of juice you use to make a more jiggly concoction. What can you do to make a more rigid concoction?

SCIENCE SPEAK

Everything is made from molecules (see page 15). But plastic molecules, called *polymers*, are special. Polymers are actually long chains of smaller molecules stuck together. In fact *poly* means many and *mer* means unit. So polymers are made of many repeating molecule units.

The Principle of the Thing

Gelatin molecules are polymers. They form a pattern that looks like a web of empty cage-like cells. When you heat them in water, the pattern breaks apart. When you cool them, the molecules form their cage pattern again, only this time something special happens. The gelatin molecules form around a water droplet so liquid water is trapped inside a solid gelatin cage! Although the concoction is jiggly, it no longer flows like a liquid. By trapping a liquid in a solid, you've created a special colloid called a *gel*.

HEATED

COOLED

When you evenly scatter bits of one substance throughout another, you create a *colloid*. Colloid particles are much smaller than those of a suspension (see page 121). Colloids can be made from any form of matter floating in another. Think about these interesting combinations:

Gels. Liquid floating in a solid. Gelatin floats liquid (water droplets) in a solid (protein).

Aerosols. Liquid floating in gas. Fog floats liquid (water droplets) in a gas (air).

Foams. Gas floating in liquid. Whipped cream floats gas (air) in a liquid (cream).

Emulsions. Liquid floating in another liquid. Mayonnaise (see page 89) floats one liquid (oil) in another (vinegar). Milk is an emulsion, too (see page 114).

GELS   AEROSOLS   FOAMS   EMULSIONS

A Life-Building Chemical

Protein—found in foods such as meat, milk, eggs, and nuts— is a substance that our body needs for growth. Proteins are made of long chains of molecules. Making gelatin causes these chains to tangle into a water-catching web.

More Fabulous Formulas

Gela-drop. Place a package of flavored gelatin mix in a glass. Use a new medicine-style dropper to place a drop of water in the center. Wait until it's absorbed. Add about 5 more drops of water in the same way to the same spot. Swirl the glass and watch a Gela-drop appear! Lift it out with a fork.

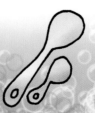

Gela-juice. Ask a grownup to help you boil 1 cup (250 ml) of your favorite juice (not pineapple) over a packet of unflavored gelatin. Stir until it's dissolved. Add 1 cup (250 ml) cold juice. Chill until firm. Enjoy!

HOT! GET HELP!

Gela-glue. Mix 2 tablespoons (25 ml) of boiling water with 1 tablespoon (15 ml) flavored gelatin for sticky glue. To make your own sticker, brush it onto the back of a small picture and let it dry. When you lick the back, it will become sticky again.

Gela-lotion. Ask a grownup to add 1 cup (250 ml) boiling water to a packet of unflavored gelatin. Stir to dissolve. Add 1 cup (250 ml) cold water; let cool. Then, stir in 2 tablespoons (25 ml) of rubbing alcohol and a dash of fragrance or vanilla. Refrigerate until it begins to thicken. Use an egg beater to whip it every half- hour or so until it resembles hand lotion. Store in the refrigerator labeled, "Do Not Eat!" Give this refreshing natural lotion as a lovely gift.

WHAT ON EARTH? Chicken-ELL-o!

Have you ever noticed the puddle of jelly around a cold chicken from last night's dinner? Where did it come from? Chew on the crunchy stuff at the end of a chicken bone while you contemplate the answer and you've discovered it— gristle. This connective tissue contains gelatin. When it's cooked, the gelatin seeps out of the gristle and mixes with the meat juices. As the mixture cools, the gelatin molecules arrange themselves in a juice-trapping pattern. It's colloidal chicken-ELL-o!

LET'S GET PRACTICAL

Gloppy Glue

Glues are made from the gelatin found in animal bones, hides, and sinews. It's even found in vegetables like Irish moss and seaweed. The gelatin is heated, processed, and dried to make a glue powder. Add water to the powder and start sticking!

BLubberScoTch

How can you change a liquid, like milk, into a glop, like pudding? Discover how the secret ingredients—heat and cornstarch—make the change.

WhaT You Need

- **Saucepan**
- **Mixing spoon**
- **Measuring cup and spoon**
- **½ cup (50 ml) brown sugar**
- **1 tablespoon (15 ml) cornstarch**
- **1 cup (250 ml) milk**

WhaT You Do

1 Stir sugar and cornstarch together in a pot.

2 Pour in a little milk; then blend until smooth. Stir in the remaining milk.

3 Ask a grownup to help you heat the mixture slowly until it's thick and bubbly.

4 Let the pudding cool; then chill in the refrigerator for about 1 hour. You've made gloppy milk—better known as pudding!

SCIENCE SPEAK

Starch is an important chemical we need in our diet. It's found in plants. Starch molecules form polymers (see page 125). When these chains become tangled, they cause liquids to thicken and gel.

The Principle of the Thing

The protein molecules of gelatin (see Jigglin' Gelatin Worms, page 124) aren't the only polymers that can gel liquid. Starch is also made of polymers in long chains of repeating sugar molecules. When cornstarch is heated in liquid, water gets inside the granules and forces the molecule chains to break lose. These loose molecule chains tangle together, trap water, and thicken the liquid to create the gel you know as pudding!

- **Cool it.** How did the pudding change after it was refrigerated? How does cooling affect this gel?

- **Slime it.** Will cornstarch gel water as well as milk? Make a disgusting slime and see. Follow the formula again but make these changes: Use water instead of milk. Use white sugar instead of brown. Add a few drops of green food coloring.

Starched Designs

SUPER FUN!

What's the main ingredient in clothes-stiffening liquid starch? Cornstarch! Make your own starchy liquid to stiffen string in a pretty design. Soak string (it can be the beautiful string you made on page 100) in slime (see More to Explore on this page; make it leaving out the sugar and coloring). Coil it into a pretty shape on a plate. Remove with a spatula. Set in the sun until dry. How has the cornstarch changed the string? You can also coil it on colored tissue paper. Cut around the outer edge of the shape for a colorful ornament.

MORE FABULOUS FORMULAS

$E = mc^2$

Experiment with other gel-producing ingredients:

 HOT! GET HELP!

 O.K. TO EAT!

Tapioca. The root of the shrubby Manioc plant has been an important food for the people of Brazil since prehistoric times. The root is a source of tapioca, a starchy thickener similar to cornstarch. You can gel milk, changing it from a liquid to a glop with this formula for tapioca pudding.

Mix 2½ cups (625 ml) milk with ¼ cup (75 ml) sugar and 3 tablespoons (40 ml) instant tapioca in a pot. Let sit for 5 minutes. Ask a grownup to heat the mixture until it boils. Remove from the heat and observe what happens over the next 20 minutes. Enjoy warm or cool.

Pectin. Pectin comes from certain fruits like apples. When cooked, it gels sugar and fruit into jams and jellies. Cranberries are so naturally pectin-rich that they gel themselves when cooked.

Ask a grownup to help you boil 1 cup (250 ml) sugar and 1 cup (250 ml) water. Add a 12-ounce (375 g) package of fresh cranberries and continue boiling gently for about 10 minutes or until berries pop. Cover and cool at room temperature. Enjoy your thickened sauce.

Thixotropy Art

This paint stays put until you push it across the paper or squeeze it from a bag.
A liquid that flows only when you push or squeeze it? That's a thixotropic fluid!

What You Need

- **Saucepan**
- **Measuring cup and spoon**
- **¼ cup (50 ml) cornstarch**
- **¾ cup (175 ml) water**
- **Paper cups**
- **Food coloring or powdered tempera dissolved in a little water**
- **Paper**
- **Plastic sandwich bags**

What You Do

1 In a pot, blend cornstarch with a little of the water until you have a smooth paste. Stir in the remaining water.

2 Ask a grownup to help you stir the mixture over low heat. Don't let it stick to the saucepan.

3 Simmer until clear and thick; then cool.

4 Divide into paper cups and blend in colorings.

Now Push . . .

Spoon globs of different colors onto paper. Observe how they just sit there! How can you get the colors to move across the page? Push them with your fingers. You're finger painting with a thixotropic fluid!

Or Squeeze . . .

Place a glob of color in the corner of a plastic sandwich bag; then snip a small hole in the corner. Observe how the color just sits there! How can you get it to flow from the bag to your painting? Squeeze the bag. You're squeeze-painting with a thixotropic fluid!

SCIENCE SPEAK

The word *thixotropy* comes from the Greek word *thixis* meaning, to touch. A thixotropic substance moves only when disturbed or touched. Apply force and it flows. Stop the force and it stays still. Strange stuff!

Most fluids flow without help, but not thixotropic fluids! They won't budge until they're pushed or squeezed. It's pressure that does the trick. Push your paints around and they flow like a liquid; stop the force and they stay put like a solid. It makes sense that gels, like this paint and Blubberscotch (page 128) are generally thixotropic. Afterall, it's their liquid water content that lets them flow when pushed and their solid cornstarch content that holds them still when they're at rest.

LET'S GET PRACTICAL

They're ALL Around

Be a thixotropic detective. Lots of thixotropic fluids are lurking in your house. Check out the refrigerator. Do you notice how the mayonnaise sits there in the jar, so smug? You can change that by simply spreading it all over a slice of bread. On to the bathroom. Take note of the toothpaste tube. Take off the cap and wait awhile. The toothpaste refuses to comes out. But squeeze that tube and in one splat, the toothpaste flows onto your brush. You've discovered thixotropy.

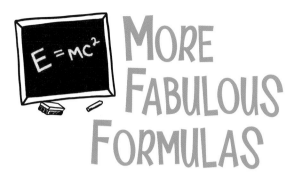

MORE FABULOUS FORMULAS

$E = mc^2$

Have more thixotropic art fun with these cornstarch concoctions:

Paste. Mix ½ cup (125 ml) cornstarch with 2 tablespoons (25 ml) of sugar in a pot. Measure out 1 cup (250 ml) of cold water. Add a little of the water and stir until smooth. Gradually add the rest of the water and stir. Ask a grownup to help you cook the mixture until it looks like paste. Cool before using.

HOT! GET HELP!

Dough. Combine 1 cup (250 ml) cornstarch with 2 cups (500 ml) baking soda and 1¼ cups (300 ml) water in a pot. Ask a grownup to help you

HOT! GET HELP!

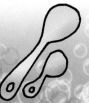

stir the mixture over low heat. When the mixture looks like mashed potatoes, remove from heat. Gather with a spoon and flop out onto a floured surface. When cool, knead until smooth.

Face paint. For each color, mix 1 teaspoon (5 ml) cornstarch, ½ teaspoon (2 ml) cold cream, and ½ teaspoon (2 ml) water in a film canister. Add a few drops of food coloring and stir until evenly blended.

Thixotropic Quicksand

WHAT ON EARTH?

Have you ever noticed when you run along a beach how the sand supports your weight? What happens when the sand becomes too watery? It won't support your weight, will it? We say the sand becomes "quick," or "alive."

Quicksand forms near mouths of rivers or flat shores where there is hard-packed clay underneath. All that water and rounded grains of sand make the sand flow, or behave, like a liquid. But unlike the quicksand in the movies, real quicksand has no sucking force.

Quicksand is even more dense than salt water (see page 75), so you know if you can float in the ocean, you can float your way out of quicksand. Like all thixotropic fluids, the more you stir up quicksand, the more liquid and less supportive it becomes. So move slowly or stand still, and you will "float" out of quicksand!

Science Clues

Is it easier to float in fresh water or salt water? For a clue, see Hovering Veggies, page 74.

Terrific Taffoid

What do foam rubber and taffy have in common? They're both colloids called solid foam. That means they both trap a gas (air) in a solid (sugar or plastic). It takes hard work to pack in all those little air bubbles. So, invite your scientist friends to join in making this solid foam—Terrific Taffoid—that's a treat to eat!

WhaT You Need

- **Deep pot**
- **Mixing spoon**
- **1 cup (250 ml) sugar**
- **¼ cup (50 ml) water**
- **2 tablespoons (25 ml) vinegar**
- **Candy thermometer**
- **1 tablespoon (15 ml) butter**
- **½ teaspoon (2 ml) vanilla**
- **Plate**

WhaT You Do

1 Combine the sugar, water, and vinegar in a deep pot. Clip a candy thermometer to the side of the pot. Boil to 265°F (130°C) or to the "hard-ball stage" (a drop of the mixture forms a ball in a cold glass of water).

2 Add the butter and vanilla; then pour onto a buttered plate to cool.

WARNING! This mixture gets extremely hot. A grownup MUST do the cooking.

3 Don't rush the cooling process. This concoction may be cool on the surface, but burning hot inside. Don't touch until a grownup tells you it is completely cooled. Then, butter your hands and work the mixture into a ball. Twist off pieces and place them in the buttered hands of your friends.

4 The basic taffy pulling movements are: pull, fold, and twist. Your goal is to work as much air into the mixture as possible. You are not making hard lollipops; you're making soft, light taffy!

5 The taffy is done when it becomes a creamy color and difficult to pull.

6 Finish it off by pulling it into a ½-inch (1 cm) thick "rope." Snip into bite-sized pieces. Wrap in waxed paper squares, twisted at each end. A jar of taffy makes a great gift—especially when you add a bit of scientific explanation!

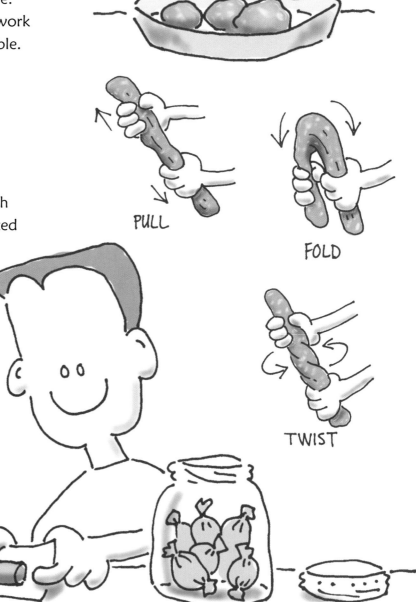

PULL

FOLD

TWIST

Sir Isaac Newton Said . . .

Only a change in temperature can change the ability of a substance to flow. Think of honey on a cold day. It doesn't budge. Now heat it up and watch the action. It flows all over the place! It's Newtonian. But what about taffy? It also refuses to budge. How did you get it to move? Not with heat, but with pressure. All that squeezing and pulling forces taffy to flow. So taffy is non-Newtonian (and thixotropic)!

The Principle of the Thing

Taffy is a colloid called *solid foam* that traps air (a gas) in sugar (a solid). The air keeps the sugar from solidifying rock hard. You mix air bubbles into the sugar by continually stretching and folding the candy. You know the air is there when you see the candy turn creamy-colored and feel it become more flexible.

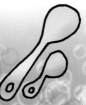

MORE FABULOUS FORMULAS

Marshmalloids. Trap some air in gelatin to make a delicious solid foam colloid, better known as marshmallow. Ask a grownup to dissolve 2 packages of unflavored gelatin in 1 cup (250 ml) of boiling water. Add 1 cup (250 ml) sugar and 2 teaspoons (10 ml) vanilla. Beat with an egg beater for about 20 minutes until the mixture looks like marshmallow cream. Place greased waxed paper in a pan and spread the mixture on top. Let it stand overnight in a kitchen cabinet. Cut into squares and roll in powdered sugar. Enjoy!

HOT! GET HELP!

O.K. TO EAT!

WHAT ON EARTH?

Sea Foam

You can work air bubbles into egg whites (meringue), sugar (taffy), and gelatin (marshmallows). Nature does the same by working air bubbles into ocean water. When waves crash on the shore, millions of tiny bubbles form as air mixes with ocean water. So when you see white sea foam, you're looking at a colloid made from air and water.

Puffy Protein Meringue

Stretch protein molecules. Fill them with air until they become light and fluffy—then eat them!

What You Need

- **4 egg whites**
- **Large mixing bowl**
- **Egg beater or whisk**
- **1 cup (250 ml) powdered sugar**
- **½ teaspoon (2 ml) cream of tartar**
- **1 teaspoon (5 ml) vanilla extract**
- **Cookie sheets**

What You Do

1 Get ready by allowing the eggs to warm to room temperature. Ask a grownup to preheat the oven to 225°F (100°C), and grease the baking sheets.

2 Place egg whites in the bowl (refrigerate yolks for French toast) and beat until they are white and foamy.

3 Add the sugar, about a tablespoon (15 ml) at a time, as you beat. Don't stop until the foam is stiff enough to stand up in little peaks. Add cream of tartar and vanilla and beat again.

4 Use a tablespoon to drop dollops of the mixture onto the baking sheet.

5 Bake for about 1 hour or until meringue feels dry. Let cool about 5 minutes before removing from the sheet.

HOT! GET HELP!

Your Puffy Proteins don't look anything like the slimy egg whites they once were. Egg whites are made mostly of proteins (see page 126). Changing the shape of protein molecule chains is easy; just beat them and they become a tangled mass that fills with air. The molecule mass stretches and tangles even more in the oven where hot air expands the air inside its spaces. That's why the meringue puffs up. By trapping air in a solid, you've discovered another way to create a solid foam colloid.

EGG PROTEIN MOLECULES

BEATEN:

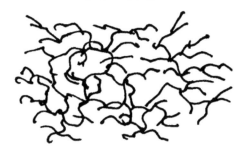

HEATED:

Science Clues

Why does hot air expand? See page 79 for a clue.

SCIENCE SPEAK

Coagulation is a special kind of chemical change (see page 51). It can happen when heat causes a liquid to change to a solid. The egg whites of the Puffy Proteins coagulate as they change from a liquid slime to a solid meringue.

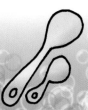
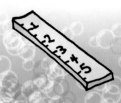

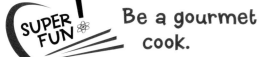 **Be a gourmet cook.**

In step 3, (page 139), add 2 teaspoons (10 ml) almond, maple, cinnamon, chocolate, or whatever flavoring suits your taste buds. Or gently fold in ½ cup (125 ml) shredded coconut or ½ cup (125 ml) chocolate chips after step 4.

Be a gourmet artist.
Add a few drops of food coloring along with the vanilla to make colorful Puffy Proteins. Then, add miniature candy-coated chocolate "eyes" for Puffy Protein creatures. Or fill a plastic baggie with the puffy mixture; snip the corner; then squeeze to form simple shapes, letters, or numbers on the baking sheet.

MORE TO EXPLORE

- Place a metal frying pan in the direct sun on a very hot summer day. Let it get very hot; then crack an egg on the surface. Will it coagulate?
- Watch as a grownup fries a sunny-side-up egg. Which coagulates first, the white or the yolk?

WHAT ON EARTH? Eggs not only make great omelets, they also make a great place for a developing chick.

Have you ever noticed the membrane on the inside of an egg shell? It's an amazing "skin" that keeps the liquid in the egg while letting air flow in and out. The egg white, or *albumen*, is a slimy cushion that protects the yolk, which is held in place by thin stringy chords attached to each end of the shell. Carefully crack an egg over a plate and look for these parts. Can you find the end of the shell where the membrane forms an air bubble? That's where the chick gets its first breath of air.

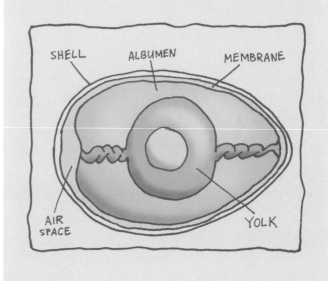

SHELL · ALBUMEN · MEMBRANE · AIR SPACE · YOLK

Sci-ICE-ence Cream

Here's your chance to explore the science and taste of homemade ice cream even if you don't own an ice-cream maker. You'll discover why ice cream is light and fluffy instead of rock solid like an ice cube.

What You Need

- **1-gallon (4 l) plastic milk jug**
- **Scissors**
- **12-ounce coffee can (or similar size can with a plastic lid)**
- **Towel**
- **1 cup (250 ml) milk**
- **1 cup (250 ml) cream**
- **½ cup (125 ml) sugar**
- **½ teaspoon (2 ml) vanilla**
- **Crushed ice**
- **Salt**
- **Wooden mixing spoon**

What You Do

1 Ask a grownup to cut the jug, as shown. Check to see that the can fits inside.

2 Wrap the jug with a towel.

3 Combine the milk, cream, sugar, and vanilla in the can.

4 Seal the can to keep salted ice from spilling inside. Then place the can into the jug.

5 Pack crushed ice around and under the can. Sprinkle the ice with salt as you pack.

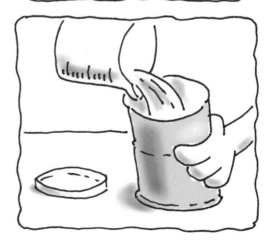

6 Remove the lid and find a partner to share in the stirring because it takes about half an hour. Be careful not to get ice or salt in the can. Use your spoon to scrape the ice cream that first forms along the sides and bottom back into the mixture.

7 When all of the mixture is slushy, serve and enjoy!

Tip: Speed things up by placing the can of liquid in the freezer for about an hour before starting.

You just kept a liquid from freezing normally! As a liquid reaches the freezing point, it becomes mushy. Then it becomes very hard. Freezing your mixture without stirring would result in a solid chunk of cream that could break your teeth!

By keeping your ice-cream mixture on the move, you break up the ice into small particles. These particles freeze individually instead of as one solid block. The more the liquid moves as it freezes, the smaller the ice particles and the smoother your ice cream will be.

Stirring also adds a secret ingredient—air—that makes ice cream light! And by trapping air in a creamy liquid you've concocted a "double colloid." It's an emulsion because cream is fat suspended in water. It's a foam because you've trapped air in the cream. So keep on stirring!

SUPER FUN! FOOL WITH FLAVORS O.K. TO EAT!

Chocolate ice cream. Add chocolate syrup.

New flavors. Substitute maple, almond, mint, or other flavorings for vanilla.

Special treats. Jazz up basic vanilla ice cream. Blend in ½ cup (125 ml) chopped fruit, ¼ cup (50 ml) chopped nuts, ¼ cup (50 ml) chocolate chips, or 1 crushed candy bar after the cream begins to thicken.

Frozen yogurt. Substitute flavored yogurt for milk, cream, sugar, and vanilla.

Slush. Freeze fruit juice.

Sherbet. Freeze 1 cup (250 ml) milk or cream, 1 cup (250 ml) fruit juice, ⅓ cup (75 ml) sugar.

WHAT ON EARTH?

Deep Freeze

Why add salt? Well, ice melts because it absorbs (takes up) heat. In this case, the ice takes heat from the cream mixture. If it can absorb enough heat, the cream will eventually freeze, which is where the salt comes in. Ordinary ice isn't cold enough to freeze cream. But salt water freezes at a lower temperature than tap water. It gets so cold, that it can absorb enough heat from the cream mixture to turn it into ice cream.

Centuries Old and Still Popular

The most delicious thing Marco Polo brought back from his trip to China 700 years ago was a recipe for "fruit-juice ices." Throughout the centuries royalty tried to guard the precious recipe, but something that good couldn't be kept from the people for long! Fruit-ice shops opened in Italy and France 300 years ago, but it was the French who thought of changing the juice to cream. Ice cream came to America in the 1700s and became one of George Washington's favorite desserts. Today the average American eats more than three gallons per year! How about you?

MORE FABULOUS FORMULAS

Baked Alaska

Bake ice cream? Impossible you say? Not so. Just protect the ice cream from the heat with a puffy jacket of meringue! Put scoops of ice cream onto thick, flat cookies. Freeze them for about an hour. Meanwhile whip up some meringue (page 138). Spread on a thick coat that covers the scoop completely—no bare spots, please! Bake for about 5 minutes at 250°F (120°C).

CUT-AWAY VIEW

The meringue's tiny air spaces slow the heat from getting to the ice cream, just as a puffy winter coat keeps your body heat in and the cold air out.

Crazy Casein

Casein is the remarkable part of milk that actually makes plastic. Here, you can make plastic similar to the way the first plastics were made about 100 years ago!

What You Need

- **½ cup (125 ml) milk**
- **1 tablespoon (15 ml) vinegar**
- **Saucepan**
- **Sieve**
- **Bowl**

What You Do

1 Pour the milk and vinegar in a saucepan.

2 Ask a grownup to help you heat it slowly; keep stirring until lumps form.

HOT!
GET HELP!

3 Remove from the stove and continue stirring until white lumps (curds) float in clear liquid (whey).

4 Strain out the lumps and place them in a bowl until cool. Gather them in your hand and rinse. Form the sticky stuff into a shape and set it out in the sun to harden.

The Principle of the Thing

Little Miss Muffet enjoyed the first step of plastic-making (and cheese-making) when she sat down to eat her curds and whey. Vinegar causes milk to separate into two parts, a liquid called whey and a solid protein curd called *casein*. The polymers (see page 125) that form casein are linked together making it moldable and plastic.

MORE TO EXPLORE

Try making casein using whole, 2%, and then skim milk. How do the results differ? Which makes the best plastic? Which makes the best glue or spread (see page 127)?

Plastics are synthetic (man-made) materials made of polymers. They are easily molded into shapes. There are two main groups of plastics. The polymers of rigid plastics tangle in a way that forms something hard and stiff, like a Frisbee. The polymers of flexible plastics can slip around each other and create something soft and bendable, like a balloon.

ARF!

WAAA !!

MORE FABULOUS FORMULAS

Glue glop. Make glue from the casein. Add 1 tablespoon (15 ml) of water and 1 teaspoon (5 ml) of baking soda to the strained lumps. Observe the chemical reaction (see page 53) as tiny bubbles form. The baking soda neutralizes the vinegar (see page 61) and leaves a wonderfully strong glue. Store in an airtight jar and refrigerate.

Casein glue is incredibly strong. It can hold more than paper. Recycle scraps of wood into junk art sculpture or make models; then use Glue Glop to hold the pieces together. Let the glue dry and admire your results.

Science spread. Making casein is the first step in cheese-making. You can eat your curds by adding a spoonful of yogurt and a dash of your favorite seasoning salt. Mash with a fork and spread on crackers. Delicious!

SUPER FUN! **Science magic.** After lunch at school, fill a plastic sandwich bag with water. Twist the top closed and grasp it to seal. Now as your amazed friends watch, jab your pencil all the way through the bag. Incredible, no leaks!

Tip: Try this at home first to be sure your bag is made from the right sort of plastic.

After the "magic," impress your friends with some science. Your bag is made from a plastic called polyethylene. One of its unusual properties is that it shrinks when torn. So, it shrinks around the pencil and keeps the water from leaking. Can you think why this plastic could be useful in making tires?

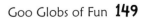

ECO-SCIENTIST

Originally plastics were made of natural substances like casein. Today, most are made from petroleum.

While your casein plastic will decompose, petroleum plastics do not. Luckily, petroleum plastics can be recycled into new products. That picnic bench in the park or the pillow on your bed may once have been milk jugs! The key to recycling is sorting plastic by type.

Look on the bottom of a plastic milk jug or soda pop bottle for the number one surrounded by the recycling symbol. This means it's made of a recyclable plastic called *polyethylene terephthalate*. Contact the waste management department of your area to find out which kinds of plastic packaging can be recycled where you live.

Some Items to Recycle:

| soft drink bottles, cassette tapes | milk jugs, detergent bottles, flower pots | tile, credit cards, sewer pipes |

WHAT ON EARTH?

Elastic Plastic, Naturally

Break the stem of a milkweed or a dandelion plant in early spring and coat your fingertip with the sap. Let it dry for a few minutes. Gently roll it off your finger and you will have made a tiny, natural rubber band! Like the latex sap of the rubber tree, dandelion sap produces a stretchy, plastic substance.

LET'S GET PRACTICAL

The Gooey Chewy

For thousands of years people have enjoyed chewing gum. Tree sap was an ancient favorite. Later, folks tried wax. What makes chewing-gum chewy is a gum base that won't dissolve. In the 1800s, gum base came from chicle of the Mexican sapodilla tree. Today's bases are made from rubber and even plastic! Of course, sugars, flavorings, and softeners are added too.

Blobber

Bend it, bounce it, even blow it up like a balloon! Discover why your concoction of the plastic Blobber is so moldable and flexible.

What You Need

- **2 paper cups**
- **½ teaspoon (2 ml) borax**
- **½ cup (125 ml) water**
- **1 tablespoon (15 ml) white glue**
- **Food coloring (optional)**

What You Do

1 In one cup, dissolve the borax in the water.

2 Pour the white glue into another cup. If you like, add about 4 drops of food coloring.

3 Add 1 tablespoon (15 ml) of the borax solution to the glue and stir with a stick or spoon.

4 Take the mixture out of the cup and knead it with your hands for several minutes. You've got Blobber!

PLaSTiC MoLeCuLeS

Everything is made from molecules. Plastic molecules, or polymers, are long chains of smaller, repeating molecules stuck together. Polymer chains can be linked, which is just what you did when you made Blobber. These long chains of cross-linked molecules are what makes plastic strong and moldable.

The Principle of the Thing

White glue is made up of millions of polymers. When polymers are dissolved in water (as in glue), they slide around each other allowing the glue to flow. They are so long, however, they get in each other's way, making the glue more viscous (flows more slowly) than water.

When you add borax solution to the glue, the polymers change. The borax cross-links, or connects (so instead of separate chains picture something more like a net). The more the polymers tangle, the more water they trap, giving Blobber that jelly-like feel. Tangled molecule chains are more difficult to pour than individual molecule chains, so Blobber is even more viscous than glue!

Unlike your Jigglin' Gelatin Worms that liquefied when heated (see page 124), Blobber is here to stay. You created a chemical reaction by mixing borax solution with glue.

Glue, water, and borax. If you change the proportions of just one of these ingredients, the amount of "rungs" or cross-linking of polymer strands changes and the Blobber behaves differently. Experiment by varying the strength of the borax solution. Give each Blobber a different color so you can tell one from another.

Follow the directions for Blobber, but change the strength of the borax solutions as follows by changing the amount of borax you add to ½ cup (125 ml) of water:

Red Blobber: 1 tsp.
Blue Blobber: ½ tsp.
Yellow Blobber: ¼ tsp.

Give them the "kid test" in Curious Kids Can.

 **CURIOUS KIDS CAN**

The Best Blobber

You are a chemist for a toy manufacturer. Your job is to produce the perfect Blobber for kids to enjoy. Do kids want to blow Blobber bubbles or would they prefer a toy they can bounce? Do they want something oozy or something stretchy? Put your Blobbers to the test to decide the kid-pleasingest Blobber (your job depends on it!).

Roll the red, yellow, and blue Blobber into equal-sized balls. Then:

Set them down. Do they ooze or hold their shape?
Press a coin on top. How long does the image last?
Squeeze. How long does your fist print last?
Bounce them. How high do they go?

Insert a straw. Seal off the Blobber by holding it tightly around the straw. Can any be used to blow a plastic bubble?

Roll Blobber into equal-sized cylinders. Then:

Stretch them to equal lengths. Wait a few seconds. How short will they shrink?
Stretch them each over a yard or meter stick. How long will they stretch?

Now, you are an adverting agent. Play with the Blobber, test it on some kids, and then design and write an ad for Blobber.

A Blob in The Hand

Surprise a friend by creating Blobber right in her hand! First have her wet her hand. Next squirt a small amount of glue onto her palm. Add a few specks of borax. Now have her rub her palms together. Voila . . . Blobber!

A Mistake That Paid Off

Try as he might, the chemist James Wright was never able to create rubber in the laboratory. But one of his mistakes did become a very popular toy. When he added boric acid to silicone oil he created a bouncing solid that oozed like a liquid. You probably know it as Silly Putty®!

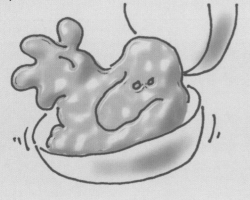

Make a Polymer-Model Necklace

SUPER FUN

Using a needle, thread gumdrops onto thread. Stitch back through each gumdrop to hold in place, spacing each one about 2 inches (5 cm) apart. Each gumdrop represents a molecule. Threaded together they model a chain of molecules, or a polymer.

Make a second chain. Now cross-link the polymer chains by threading a strand from a gumdrop on one chain to a gumdrop on the other chain, like rungs on a ladder. Now you've made a model of a cross-linked polymer, like Blobber. Tie it around your neck and you've got wearable science art!

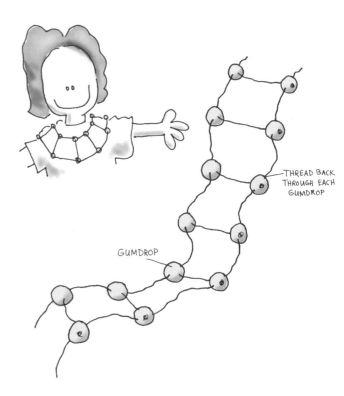

THREAD BACK THROUGH EACH GUMDROP

GUMDROP

MORE FABULOUS FORMULAS

If you have a contact lens wearer in your family, you can cross-link polymers to make slime and plastic film. Look for *polyvinyl alcohol* listed as an ingredient of contact lens wetting solution (less expensive generic brands work well).

Slime. Mix ½ teaspoon (2 ml) of borax in ½ cup (125 ml) water. In a clear film canister, add 2 teaspoons (10 ml) of this solution to 1 tablespoon (15 ml) of wetting solution. Shake; then pour onto your hand.

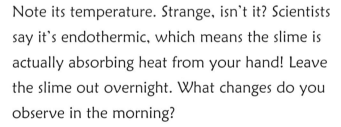

Note its temperature. Strange, isn't it? Scientists say it's endothermic, which means the slime is actually absorbing heat from your hand! Leave the slime out overnight. What changes do you observe in the morning?

Plastic film. Pour a thin layer of slime onto a metal jar lid. Leave it in a warm spot until it dries out (several hours). Can you peel off the plastic film that remains? What happens if you wet the film?

PLENTIFUL PLASTIC

Imagine a substance that can be rigid like a soda pop bottle or flexible like a balloon. It can be transparent like a contact lens or opaque like a toothpaste tube. What is this strange stuff? Plastic! From Frisbees to Velcro, from white glue to windshield wipers—plastics take almost every imaginable form. How can plastics be so different? The answer has to do with the different kinds of molecules that make up plastic and the way those molecules are linked together.

Index

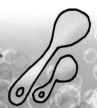

More Good Children's Books from Williamson Books

Williamson Books are available from your bookseller or directly from Ideals Publications. Please see last page for contact and ordering information.

Also by Jill Frankel Hauser:

THE KIDS' GUIDE TO BECOMING THE BEST YOU CAN BE!
Developing 5 Traits You Need to Achieve Your Personal Best

American Bookseller Pick of the Lists
Benjamin Franklin Best Education/Teaching Award
American Institute of Physics Science Writing Award
Parents' Choice Honor Award
GIZMOS & GADGETS
Creating Science Contraptions that Work (& Knowing Why)

American Bookseller Pick of the Lists
Dr. Toy Best Vacation Product
KIDS' CRAZY ART CONCOCTIONS
50 Mysterious Mixtures for Art & Craft Fun

SCIENCE PLAY
Beginning Discoveries for 2- to 6-Year-Olds

KINDERGARTEN SUCCESS
Helping Children Excel Right from the Start

WOW! I'M READING!
Fun Activities to Make Reading Happen

KIDS CARE!
75 Ways to Make a Difference for People, Animals & the Environment
by Rebecca Olien

MAKING AMAZING ART!
40 Activities Using the 7 Elements of Art Design
by Sandi Henry

AWESOME OCEAN SCIENCE
Investigating the Secrets of the Underwater World
by Cindy A. Littlefield

LIGHTHOUSES OF NORTH AMERICA!
Exploring Their History, Lore & Science
by Lisa Trumbauer

TALES ALIVE!
Ten Multicultural Folktales with Activities
by Susan Milord

American Bookseller Pick of the Lists
Skipping Stones Nature & Ecology Honor Award
ECOART!
Earth-Friendly Art & Craft Experiences for 3- to 9-Year-Olds
by Laurie Carlson

Learning Magazine Teachers' Choice Award
KIDS' EASY-TO-CREATE WILDLIFE HABITATS
For Small Spaces in City, Suburb, Countryside
by Emily Stetson

Parents' Choice Gold Award
Dr. Toy Best Vacation Product
THE KIDS' NATURE BOOK
365 Indoor/Outdoor Activities & Experiences
by Susan Milord
Skipping Stones Nature & Ecology Honor Award
Parents' Choice Honor Award
The National Parenting Center Seal of Approval Award

MONARCH MAGIC
Butterfly Activities & Nature Discoveries
by Lynn M. Rosenblatt

Parents' Choice Recommended
THE KIDS' BOOK OF WEATHER FORECASTING
Build a Weather Station, "Read" the Sky & Make Predictions!
by Mark Breen & Kathleen Friestad

Children's Digest Health Education Award
Parents' Choice Recommended
ForeWord Magazine Book of the Year Honorable Mention
THE KIDS' GUIDE TO FIRST AID
All about Bruises, Burns, Stings, Sprains & Other Ouches
by Karen Buhler Gale, R.N.

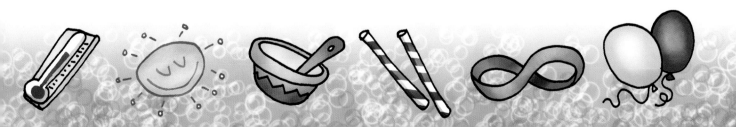